RELIGION IN MODERN SOCIETIES

In *Religion in Modern Societies*, Gunnar Skirbekk examines the challenging relationship between religion, science, and the state, and explores literature on religion in Western and Muslim-majority societies.

Through the lens of modernity theory and the perspective of philosophy of science, key issues are discussed, including freedom of expression and the interaction between religion and modern institutions. Chapters include:

- Science and Religion
- The Problem of Evil
- Freedom of Expression
- Multiculturalism and the Welfare State
- Religion as Social Integration
- Islam in a Historical Class Perspective

The topics discussed are universal issues which in principle hold relevance for all of us living in a modern science-based world and societies in crisis.

This volume is essential reading to those with an interest in philosophy of religion, religion and science, the work of Jürgen Habermas, the theory of modernization, and the politicization of religion.

Gunnar Skirbekk is a professor of philosophy, now emeritus, at the Department of Philosophy and the Center for the Study of the Sciences and the Humanities, University of Bergen, Norway.

RELIGION IN MODERN SOCIETIES

Gunnar Skirbekk

LONDON AND NEW YORK

First published 2024
by Routledge
4 Park Square, Milton Park, Abingdon, Oxon OX14 4RN

and by Routledge
605 Third Avenue, New York, NY 10158

Routledge is an imprint of the Taylor & Francis Group, an informa business

© 2024 Gunnar Skirbekk

The right of Gunnar Skirbekk to be identified as author of this work
has been asserted in accordance with sections 77 and 78 of the
Copyright, Designs and Patents Act 1988.

All rights reserved. No part of this book may be reprinted or
reproduced or utilised in any form or by any electronic, mechanical, or
other means, now known or hereafter invented, including
photocopying and recording, or in any information storage or retrieval
system, without permission in writing from the publishers.

Trademark notice: Product or corporate names may be trademarks or
registered trademarks, and are used only for identification and
explanation without intent to infringe.

Original version: *Religion i moderne samfunn*, Dreyers forlag, Oslo
2021, translated by Dr. Helene Nilsen, at the University of Bergen, and
adapted for an international audience.

British Library Cataloguing-in-Publication Data
A catalogue record for this book is available from the British Library

ISBN: 978-1-032-57920-7 (hbk)
ISBN: 978-1-032-57922-1 (pbk)
ISBN: 978-1-003-44161-8 (ebk)

DOI: 10.4324/9781003441618

Typeset in Sabon
by SPi Technologies India Pvt Ltd (Straive)

In memory of Walid al-Kubaisi (1958–2018),
friend and secular citizen,
who gave me a magnificent edition of the Qur'an.

CONTENTS

Preface	*ix*
Introduction	*x*

PART I
Science and religion   **1**

1 Eight points about science and religion in modern science-based societies in crisis   3

2 To speak of God in the light of the problem of evil   19

PART II
Religion and the constitutional state   **35**

3 Freedom of expression and cartoons   37

4 Offence, the limit of freedom of expression?   52

PART III
Religion and modern institutions   **55**

5 Multiculturalism and the welfare state?   57

viii Contents

PART IV
Religion in modern societies   **75**

6 Religion as social integration   77
   Jürgen Habermas

7 Islam in a historical class perspective   97
   Ahmet T. Kuru

8 Religion in science-based and institutionally
   differentiated societies in crisis: Concluding remarks   108

Info on previous work   *111*
Index   *112*

PREFACE

This book is a collection of texts on religion in modern societies. It is structured to facilitate a consecutive reading from beginning to end. However, the various parts are also composed in a way that makes it possible to read them one by one and independently of each other.

The texts are generally rather brief, often with many footnotes. This is a conscious choice, on my part. I wanted the book to be fair to read also for those with little time for extensive reading. At the same time, the book offers a number of footnotes for those who want to check the references and seek further clarification. These references and clarifications are crucial for the scholarly credibility of the book as a whole. But if I had included them in the text itself, I am afraid it would have made the book less accessible for those with little time for extensive reading.

I would like to thank friends and colleagues for useful feedback on the work with these texts.

Religion in modern societies – the topic invokes energetic discussion. Temperatures are high. And rightly so. Because it is, in several ways, an important topic. So, here is my contribution to the current debate on religion in modern societies.

G.S.

INTRODUCTION

I have long been interested in religion and theology, as is clear from the first book I wrote (*Nihilism?* from 1958). At the time, I reacted against a vulgar criticism of religion, such as the kind that was flourishing in a combination of literary rhetoric and outdated positivism. At the same time, I was quite concerned about the problem of evil, in theology as well.[1]

A lot is being said about religion in our time, from different perspectives. The topic of this book is "religion in modern societies", and the take is one of modernity theory[2] from a perspective of the philosophy of science.[3] The first part discusses the relationship between *science and religion* from a theory of science perspective. This is a universal issue which in principle holds relevance

---

1 The opening words in the Norwegian article "Behovet for ei modernisering av medvitet og dermed for sjølvkritisk rasjonalitetskritikk og religionskritikk», [«The need for a modernization of consciousness and thus for a self-critical critique of rationality and of religion"] in *Religion og kultur. Ein fleirfagleg samtale*, eds. Arve Brunvoll, Hans Bringeland, Nils Gilje and Gunnar Skirbekk, Universitetsforlaget, Oslo 2009, p. 87.

2 Cf. the notion of modernity in the tradition from Max Weber (and Jürgen Habermas), which conceives of modernity (and modernization) as ongoing *differentiation and rationalization* of *institutions*, such as the state, the marked, and the lifeworld, and also science, law, and art, along with their related "*value spheres*", i.e., truth, justice, and beauty. (Roughly speaking, in early Habermas, *state* and *market* are run by power in terms of strategic rationality, and the "*lifeworld*" is ruled by communicative rationality.)

3 Here, conceived as "philosophy of the sciences and the humanities"; cf. the notion "theory of the sciences and the humanities" at the *Center for the Study of the Sciences and the Humanities* at the University of Bergen: http://uib.no/en/svt/23556/theory-science and http://uib.no/en/svt/21651/history-centre.

for all of us living in a modern science-based world. The second part discusses *religion and freedom of expression* as it is acted out in modern constitutional states. This issue holds particular relevance for those living in modern science-based constitutional states. The third part discusses *religion in modern and generous welfare states*. This issue holds particular relevance for those living in modern science-based and constitutional welfare states. The fourth and last part discusses *a couple of relevant contributions* to the current discussion of *religion in modern societies*. These issues hold relevance for all living in science-based and institutionally differentiated societies in crisis.

In short, the basic topic is religion in modern societies. But first, some introductory remarks on central terms might be useful:

- *Religion* – the usage of the term is ambiguous and contested. But in our context, it should be sufficient to note that the word usually includes *at least* the three monotheistic world religions; Judaism, Christianity, and Islam – more on this later!
- *Modern societies*, again, an ambiguous expression, which we will here specify by a longer phrase, namely: *science-based and institutionally differentiated societies in crisis*.
  The following are some comments on the three central terms: *science-based*, *institutionally differentiated*, and *societies in crisis*.
- Science-based, referring to *all* sciences, and humanities, with a special focus on what they have in *common* – namely, open and enlightened discussion.
- Institutionally differentiated, the expression is used about the development of different societal institutions, with their inherent roles.
- Societies in crisis – the expression refers to a dual crisis in modern societies: *out in the world*, where different crises are often intertwined and mutually intensifying, and at the *level of knowledge*, where no singular scientific expertise may alone grasp the complexity of what is going on; the crises are not merely ecological and nature-based but also institutional and socio-cultural in various ways, and thereby also knowledge-related in different ways.

To summarize our points so far: To live in some form of a *modern science-based, institutionally differentiated society in crisis*, and particularly in a *democratic state governed by the rule of law*, potentially also in a well-functioning *welfare state*, is something with implications for how we can and should live our lives, also with regard to religion. This is precisely the point of departure for the discussions in this book, under the title *Religion in Modern Societies*, and this is what I attempt to address in the following texts.

Finally, a tip: Anyone who wants to know "what the author is up to" and "where he is coming from" is welcome to take a look under the heading "Info on Previous Work" at the end of the book.

PART I

Science and religion

1

EIGHT POINTS ABOUT SCIENCE AND RELIGION IN MODERN SCIENCE-BASED SOCIETIES IN CRISIS[1]

We live in modern science-based societies in crisis.[2] Therefore, many of us ask whether science can solve the complex and urgent challenges that we are currently facing. And many of us have questions about the relationship between science and religion in such modern societies. Big questions indeed. In this chapter, we will let it suffice to take a closer look at specific aspects of these issues. First, we will address four points concerning the role of science in modern societies. Next, we will discuss four points on the relationship between science and religion in such societies.

At the outset, we need to explain what we mean by these terms: Here I understand 'science' in the sense of '*Wissenschaft*', that is, not merely as natural science (*Naturwissenschaft*), but, broadly speaking, as *all* the disciplines at a full-scale university, from mathematics and the different disciplines within the natural sciences, to the various social sciences, psychology, and the range of disciplines within the humanities, such as linguistics and history or philosophy and comparative literature, as well as medicine, law, and theology. As a reminder I shall often use the term in plural, not 'science', but the 'sciences'. We use the word 'sciences' to refer to what these disciplines have *in common*, namely informed and self-critical argumentation, and mutual learning processes. We will return to the concept of 'religion' later in this chapter, but first, we will address the four points on science in modern societies:

---

1 This chapter is a revised version of the article "Science and religion?", in *Sacred Science? On Science and its interrelations with religious worldviews*, Simen Andersen Øyen, Tone Lund-Olsen and Nora Sørensen Vaage, (eds.), Wageningen Academic Publishers, Wageningen 2012.

2 For more on challenges in modern societies, cf. Gunnar Skirbekk, *Epistemic Challenges in a Modern World. From 'fake news' and 'post truth' to underlying epistemic challenges in science-based risk-societies*, LIT Verlag, Zürich 2019.

DOI: 10.4324/9781003441618-2

4 Science and religion

Common to all sciences: informed and self-critical argumentation, and mutual learning processes

When talking about the sciences "solving our problems" it is often assumed that the sciences are useful in an *instrumental* sense, where purposive knowledge and competence are targeted,[3] such as for improved governance and economic growth. However, not all sciences are *instrumentally useful*. The humanities are typically not useful in this sense.[4] The social relevance and usefulness of the humanities are primarily of a different kind.

Hence, instrumental usefulness, for politics or economy, cannot be a common denominator and a common legitimation for all the various sciences. They differ both when it comes to the usage of their research results and when it comes to what the researchers are doing, for instance in labs, in fieldwork, in libraries, or on research expeditions in distant regions.

Yet, in all disciplines, however different they may be from one another, researchers *in spe* have to defend their theses in a doctoral disputation. In short, it is not instrumental usefulness, but argumentative and self-critical discussion that all university disciplines have in common.

Sure enough, in practice, there are great differences in the extent and depth of the argumentative activity, not least when it comes to self-criticism and reflexivity. Moreover, in scientific communities, there is also a demand for originality, for new conceptions and perspectives, or methods and procedures, in addition to a solid practice-based professional competence and a well-founded professional discretion.

Notwithstanding all of these aspects, however, at crucial moments, a competent and professional 'give and take' of reasons is required. This requirement is not merely a matter of 'giving' – of providing relevant arguments – but also a question of being open towards relevant counterarguments and to take them seriously. For this reason, there is no place for anxious aversion towards arguments, *argumentophobia*,[5] in modern science-based societies.

This is now my first point: that which is common to all sciences, at least ideally and potentially, is not instrumental usefulness, but informed and self-critical argumentation by way of mutual learning processes.

The need for informed and self-critical criticism

Also in a broader scope, beyond the internal activities within the various disciplines, self-critical discussions are needed; this is true both for the

---

3 On the relationship between explanation, prediction and practical maxims, cf. e.g. Carl Hempel, in "The Function of General Law in History", *Journal of Philosophy*, 39: 1942, pp. 35–48.
4 Concerning the humanities, cf. "Crisis in the Humanities?", in Gunnar Skirbekk, *Timely Thoughts*, Rowman & Littlefield, Lanham 2007, pp. 23–35.
5 The term 'argumentophobia' was coined by my colleague Lars Johan Materstvedt.

relationship *between* the various disciplines and for the interface between the sciences and *society*. A few reminders: each discipline has its proper concepts and perspectives, such as in economics, ecology, sociology, political science, and psychology. Thus, each discipline (and subdiscipline) 'sees' and acknowledges some aspects of an issue while 'disregarding' and neglecting others – consider e.g. the differences in researching the 'same' phenomenon, such as marriage in modern societies, from the perspective of e.g. economy, sociology, psychology, or law. In short: each discipline (and subdiscipline) 'reveals' some phenomena and 'conceals' others. There is no 'God's eye view' that sees all things from all sides simultaneously.[6]

Now, due to the perspectivist nature of the various sciences, we may consider two major challenges in the relationship between the sciences and society, not the least for political initiatives:

a In these cases, there is always a danger that one discipline (or even subdiscipline) may acquire a predominant position (among political agents or in public awareness), at the sacrifice of other disciplines that reveal other aspects of the problems we are facing. A flagrant case is the discrepancy between the dominant position of (short-term) neoliberal economics, often in contrast to the far weaker position of (long-term) ecology, with relevance for the same issue. This kind of discrepancy is a general challenge in modern science-based societies with extensive disciplinary differentiations and specializations.

For instance, we may talk about 'economism' in cases when some economic disciplines get 'the upper hand' at the sacrifice of other relevant disciplines, about 'biologism' in similar cases for biological (or neuroscientific) disciplines, or about 'contextualism' in cases when contextualist cultural studies get a dominant position.

b Secondly, due to the perspectivist nature of the various sciences, there is also a danger that the practitioners in one field (say, nuclear physics or biochemistry) do not envision the potentially unintended consequences of their own research, a challenge that requires *other* disciplinary perspectives, e.g. from the social sciences.

This means that there is a "struggle between the faculties" (the disciplines) – not merely within multidisciplinary institutions such as universities, but also in society at large – a struggle that is often related to strong political and economic interests and power relations.[7] Hence, we should always keep a

---

6 Nor is there a kind of meta-science and meta-language that encompasses all the different conceptual and disciplinary perspectives in a higher semantic synthesis.

7 E.g. between economic interests and ecological interests (where the economic interests may be strong and short-sighted, while the ecological interests are weak and long-sighted).

6 Science and religion

critical eye on the possible unfortunate and illegitimate power-relatedness of the various scientific disciplines and on how they are used and implemented, in modern societies.[8]

With the massive growth in the number of researchers and research institutions, including published reports and results, and extensive differentiation of disciplines and specialties, it has become increasingly difficult to obtain a professional overview of what is going on in a traditional discipline. Therefore, it has become increasingly common to remain within one's own narrowly conceived professional network. Which is understandable. But this development comes with a cost. As a consequence, one avoids critical and constructively disturbing remarks from colleagues in one's own or neighbouring fields.[9] Hence, there is a risk of an increasingly narrow disciplinary focus and for a weaker self-critical awareness of one's own presumptions and limitations.

All in all, this means that there is a need for measures that may facilitate self-critical and informed discussions within multidisciplinary and research-based universities,[10] and also a need for improving the public debate about the various sciences and of their use and misuse in modern societies.

This is my second point: Due to the complex and potentially contentious scientific plurality in modern science-based societies in crisis, there is an inherent and urgent need for an informed and self-critical discussion on the different sciences, the relationship between them, and the interface between the sciences and society – in short, there is a need for informed and self-critical critique of the sciences (*Wissenschaftskritik*). This implies that members of such modern societies are not free to *reject* or *disregard* certain important and relevant scientific perspectives and disciplines. In these kinds of modern societies, there is no justification for being *semi-modern* in the sense that one accepts certain sciences but rejects or disregards others.

An inherent ethos of improvement

At the outset, Karl Popper had a clear-cut demarcation for distinguishing between science and non-science: scientific statements must be falsifiable! On

---

8 Added to this, in modern societies, we have "Big Science", based on advanced technology facilitated by strong economic agents and institutions in politics and industry. See, e.g., Jaron Lanier, *Ten Arguments for Deleting Your Social Media Account Right Now*, Vintage Publishing, London 2018.

9 Or from enlightened and interested laypeople.

10 In other words, a need for critical and informed 'theory of the sciences' as the concept was defined by the Norwegian Research Council in the 1970s; cf. *Vitenskapsteoretiske fag: rapport fra en konferanse om de vitenskapsteoretiske fags stilling i Norge*, NAVF, Oslo 1976 (see website for SVT, University of Bergen).

the other hand, we find those who emphasize scientific research as a social activity not to be neatly distinguished from other social activities.[11]

Earlier, we indicated that informed and self-critical discussion should be seen as a common denominator for all sciences, broadly defined. However, this is not a demarcation between scientific research (in the broad sense) on the one hand and other social activities on the other. In modern science- and technology-based societies, there is a wide range of science-related professions and activities, outside the realm of the academic context and research institutions, from engineering to teaching and also innumerable activities in our daily life.

Moreover, in modern democratic societies, there is a need for enlightened discussions in public space as a precondition for reasonable and fair political decisions. Furthermore, in modern pluralistic societies, where fewer activities are predetermined by a given tradition or religion, open and honest discussion with others constitutes a reasonable approach for achieving perceptions that we can trust and that we can act on as a community.[12]

In other words, science-based and science-related activities are spread out into society at large, beyond the realm of organized scientific research; moreover, in modern societies, and especially in modern democratic societies, there is an inherent (ethical) need for open and enlightened argumentation and mutual learning processes. In that sense, the idea of a *demarcation line* (between science and non-science) would be misleading, and hence we should rather talk in terms of *gradualistic transitions*.[13]

However, this does not mean that an *ideal-type distinction* between scientific and other social activities is simply obsolete (and ready to be "deconstructed" in postmodernist terminology!). To illustrate this point, we may compare this distinction with the ideal-type distinction between health and illness. While it obviously makes sense to distinguish between health and illness *conceptually*, as ideal types, we are, *at an empirical level*, for the most part, more or less healthy or more or less ill, in different ways.

Moreover, by talking in gradualistic terms, we somehow *presuppose* an analytic distinction between health and illness, and we assess our current condition, being more or less healthy or ill, in relation to these ideal types.[14]

---

11 Frankly put: As is the case for the post-modernists. Counter to this, Robert Merton had his ideal-type norms for scientific research (the CUDOS, the scientific ethos; rephrased as communalism, universality, disinterestedness, and organized scepticism). Cf. *Social Theory and Social Structure*, Free Press, New York 1949.

12 Cf. John Stuart Mill, *On Liberty*, Chapter II, Of the Liberty of Thought and Discussion, 1859.

13 In short, we should talk gradualistically, not merely dichotomically.

14 When discussing freedom of speech, we acknowledge that the conversational situation may carry dimensions of manipulation and strategic choices. But this does not mean that the normative distinction between manipulative and non-manipulative conversations is irrelevant or invalid. On the contrary, it is through this distinction (of ideal types) that we are able to assess the normative status and the relative presence of manipulation in the conversational situation.

8 Science and religion

The distinction between the positive and the negative might take us a step further: In many cases, our concern is that of *avoiding* the negative (e.g. a specific disease or injury), rather than that of *achieving* some form of perfection (e.g. a perfect health – whatever *that* might be).[15] In so far, the point is that of getting away from some specific evil, seen as negative, steering towards improvement – in practice, a gradualistic and melioristic process.

In this respect, we could recognize something similar in scientific activities but also, in more general terms, in cases of enlightened and open discussions among fallible and reasonable persons: In such cases, we strive for *more well-founded* opinions, by *moving away from* less good reasons, towards better reasons, where the goal is not to reach the one and final Truth, but to achieve a realistic improvement.[16]

This is my third point: The inherent ethos of enlightened and self-critical discussion does not only apply to scientific research, nor merely to scientific activities in a broader sense, but beyond this, and more generally, there is, in modern science-based and pluralistic societies, *an inherent need* of epistemic *improvement*, away from that which is conceived as less reasonable, towards that which seems to be better.[17]

Science: part of the solution, part of the problem

When the sciences are defined as they are earlier in this chapter, in what sense could they be said to "solve" the fundamental problems of modern societies in crisis?

Surely, the sciences themselves, conceived as scientific research *detached from* societal agents and institutions, can hardly solve any practical problems, only theoretical ones. But scientific competence and insight are often decisive when used in an enlightened and responsible way by enlightened and responsible actors in adequate and justifiable institutions.

Yet, a lot of urgent problems, such as those related to renewable energy and climate change, to future supply of fresh water and food, and to unsustainable consumption and reproduction, are already utterly *complex* at the *epistemic* level,[18] for instance in the sense that various disciplines are required in order to understand current (and future) events. How do we decide what kinds of discipline and knowledge are required in the various

---

15 In the Norwegian welfare state, cancer surgery and broken bones are covered by the state, while aesthetical surgery and body building are covered by the individual.

16 But this does not mean that all statements are fallible and uncertain. We know many things with reasonable certainty, and sometimes with absolute certainty. Cf. the example-based discussions in Gunnar Skirbekk, «Wahrheit und Begründung», e.g., pp. 32–33, *Philosophie der Moderne*, Velbrück Wissenschaft, Weilerswist 2017.

17 That is, *gradualistic* and *melioristic* (to stay within the disciplinary jargon).

18 Epistemic, philosophical term, from Greek: *episteme*: knowledge.

cases? How do we decide whether there is an unreasonable dominance by some disciplines and their disciplinary perspectives at the expense of other disciplines that might also contribute to a better understanding of the problem under consideration? And again, what about unintended consequences (often unimagined within one's own disciplinary perspective)? What about epistemic uncertainty of different kinds? And what about the danger of various kinds of power-related influence on research processes and research reports?

These are problems already at the *epistemic* level. Then we have the complexity and challenges at the *institutional* level, including the danger related to pressure groups and vested economic interests, and political agents, including military and religious organizations and agents. Surely, for this reason, there is a permanent need for a critical and self-critical awareness of epistemic challenges, as well as of institutional shortcomings and irregular power relations.

On the other hand, it won't work without institutions and agents. But then there is a decisive distinction between irregular power relations without fair and reasonable legitimation and power relations that are regular and regulated, for instance, by institutional division of power and the rule of law, and that can thus be seen as *legitimate* power relations.

Constitutional democracy and democratic law-making are seen as legitimate institutions fostering legitimate decisions. The paradigmatic case is a self-contained society where those who make the laws are those for whom the laws apply, and for nobody else, and where those who give the laws understand what they are doing, including the implications and long-term consequences of what they have decided. This is the principle of popular sovereignty. Laws and other major decisions are legitimate when they are agreed upon by all those concerned.[19] This is a bottom-up, not top-down legitimation, be it either by a sovereign king or by divine command.[20]

However, in modern democratic societies, this paradigmatic case of legitimate democratic decisions and legitimate democratic legislation has become more or less problematic – in short, due to three dilemmas: (i) *Space*: In a modern globalized world, decisions made in one country tend to have

---

19 "Are agreed upon", or "would be agreed upon" in a more hypothetical case? And "those concerned" understood as "all concerned", but this poses problems, both in practice and in theory. What's more, democratic decisions may be problematic in cases where minority constellations become long term. In such cases, an egalitarian and consensus-seeking culture may be beneficial, characterized by moderate socio-economic differences, fundamental solidarity, and mutual trust. In these cases, trust is a resource – in a democratic state – and here we speak of 'trustworthy trust', not 'blind faith' based in illusions and fake news. In the words of Onora O'Neill, it is a matter of 'trust' *vs.* 'trustworthiness'. See, e.g., "Linking trust to trustworthiness", *International Journal of Philosophical Studies*, 26(2), 2018, pp. 293–300.

20 The latter becomes problematic when there is more than one religion in a society, as we shall see below.

10 Science and religion

consequences and implications for citizens in other countries. As we know: decisions made in powerful states, such as the U.S. or China, may have implications for other countries and their citizens. (ii) *Time*: Due to modern science and technology, and modern institutions, quite a few of the decisions made by our generation have extensive implications and consequences for future generations. (iii) *Insight*: In complex modern risk- societies, it is not always easy to know what the consequences might be, of the various projects and arrangements introduced by agents and institutions in our generation. In short, for these three reasons, there is often a discrepancy between the paradigmatic case of legitimate democratic decisions and many of the decisions that we are making, by virtue of our status as democratic citizens.[21]

What can be done? Just to put a label on the dilemmas: (i) The first dilemma, that of space, is primarily an institutional challenge, which soon becomes a political and normative issue: What kinds of political borders are desirable and also feasible? (ii) The second dilemma, that of time, is also at the outset an institutional challenge, which likewise becomes a political and normative issue. Our Western democracies, based on frequent elections, have the great advantage that an incompetent and unpopular government can be rejected by the voting majority; but it works from a short-term perspective, without an institutional safeguard for the voices of future generations.[22] (iii) The third dilemma, that of adequate insight, is both an institutional and an epistemic challenge. For one thing, it is worthwhile recalling that modern, well-functioning democratic societies have extended and mandatory education for all citizens. This is not a coincidence. In order for a functioning democracy to have autonomous and responsible citizens, it is necessary that the general public is reasonably enlightened about the workings of the political system. In today's complex modern societies, however, this endeavour has become even more demanding – while the level of education has increased, so has the complexity. There are many reasons why it is challenging to pay attention at the level that is required for a citizen in a complex modern democracy in crisis. A brief story may illustrate the point:

It is said that at the time of the attack on the World Trade Center in New York on 9/11, a journalist heard the following utterances by two U.S. citizens watching the whole thing: "This is like Pearl Harbor", the first said. "What's that?" the second person asked. "That was when the Vietnamese attacked us and the Vietnam War started", was the reply. The point of the story is this: these were U.S. citizens with the right and responsibility of voting for the U.S. president, a mighty agent with the power to make decisions with deep and

---

21 In the sense of (*mündiger*) *Staatsbürger*.
22 The same is true of globalised capitalism, with a relatively short-term perspective for the economic profit of invested capital.

Eight points about science and religion **11**

long-term implications for many people, at home and abroad.[23] Hence, as a citizen of a democratic society – with the right to vote and speak out, with the right to organize and demonstrate – one does have some joint responsibility, certainly always according to one's own position and capabilities, and certainly only a minor part, but still, as a citizen of a democratic society one does have some joint responsibility for what is going to happen. This point has a crucial implication: an unnecessary lack of insight into the major challenges of our time is regrettable, both for the individual (depending on personal resources and positions) and for society at large, in terms of educational policy in functioning democracies. The latter means that political and social agents have an obligation to further a good common education[24] and to foster an enlightened public space.[25] The former means that each citizen (again according to personal resources) has an obligation to be reasonably updated on major issues. The libertarian ideal of a total individual freedom is outdated in modern democratic risk-societies with some degree of shared co-responsibility. This means, bluntly stated, that each citizen in a modern democratic society has a basic obligation to improve his or her own status as an enlightened and autonomous person.[26] Ideally, this would include some concern for various kinds of scientific insight and for a self-critical and argumentative approach.

Now, back to the initial question: Are the sciences able to "solve" the fundamental problems we are facing? As a response, I restrict myself to a few short remarks:

Some of the main problems in modern societies are themselves jointly determined by the sciences, by science-based projects and technologies and science-related institutions – though, in some cases due to one-sided usage and implementation. In that sense, the way in which they are put to use, are parts of the problem. But anyway, since there is no going back to a pre-modern, pre-scientific world, we cannot avoid looking at the sciences, at all the various sciences and their common self-critical culture,[27] when we, in our time, look for reasonable contributions that could be helpful in coping with urgent problems in modern societies. This goes both for our *understanding* of the current

---

23 A political actor with the authority (*inter alia*) to start wars, e.g. in Iraq and other fragile states. Therefore, it is important that North American citizens, those who elect the U.S. president, have reasonably realistic perceptions about the global situation, such as where Iraq is located and what people do there, and what might happen if one intervenes by means of armed forces, demolishes the power structures, and disarms the army.

24 In addition, it is necessary to work towards moderate socio-economic differences by trying to ensure decent employment and a decent welfare system.

25 Cf. The Norwegian Constitution Article 100, section 6.

26 In the Kantian sense of *Mündigkeit*.

27 Therefore, it is unfortunate when multidisciplinary universities, with very different disciplines, with different activities and needs, become subjected to a uniform institutional organization and to market-based funding schemes.

12 Science and religion

challenges, and for how our *institutional* arrangements and other practical measures may be helpful in addressing complex and urgent problems.[28]

So this is my fourth point: The sciences themselves cannot "solve" the complex and urgent problems we are facing, and to some extent, the sciences are themselves part of the problem. However, when used in an enlightened and self-critical way, the sciences, in all their multitudes and with their common self-critical potential, do constitute a necessary aspect of any serious attempt to understand and face the range of urgent problems in our time.

What, then, of *religion* in modern science-based societies? Here are four points:

Plurality of religions: a need for clarifying definitions and convincing justifications

In our time, there is a pluralism of religions, such as different and often opposing versions of each of the three monotheistic religions, Judaism, Christianity, and Islam, and in addition New Age, Satanism, and witchcraft (old and new), and also other world religions, such as Hinduism and Buddhism, and different forms of religious practices, with or without a belief in God or theological theses. For instance, one God, or many, or none? Is God radically separated from the world and humankind, or are there gradual transitions between God and human beings, and between God and the world? Is God benevolent, or evil, or neither? Given this pluralism, when we talk about 'religion', who then has the right to decide, for others, what is included and what is excluded?

While this is in principle a semantic point, it has extensive practical implications, both legally and politically. This open-ended, indeterminate pluralism implies that an appeal for general 'religious' rights (of a legal or economic nature) no longer has a clear and definite meaning. This also holds true for what is said about 'religion' in legal texts, such as the United Nations Universal Declaration of Human Rights.

Due to this indeterminate pluralism of 'religion', the term has to be defined, and if religion is said to deserve respect and legal rights, that has to be justified in each case, with convincing arguments. In other words, if there are special reasons why a certain religion deserves special respect and support, this has to be shown in each case by arguments that are universally understandable and convincing, that is, by universally valid arguments.

---

28 Some claim that technology and the adjacent sciences are fundamentally neutral, and that any problems are due to misuse of this technology and these sciences by incompetent or malignant actors. Others see technology and the adjacent sciences as pressing problems in their own right, as a mentality and as practice. This can be related to current debates between the techno-optimists and the techno-scepticists. Among the latter group we find, *inter alia*, Heidegger-inspired thinkers in German, French, and North-American scholarship, e.g. the early Frankfurt School in Germany, French scholars such as Dominique Janicaud and Bruno Latour, and Hubert Dreyfus among the Anglophone.

Eight points about science and religion **13**

In short, due to this semantic pluralism, the reference to something as 'religion' is in itself no reason for special respect or concern. This is my first point: In our modern societies, there is a plurality of religions of very different kinds. Hence, there is no reason for respect or support simply because something is taken to be a 'religion'. To deserve special respect and legal support, there has to be a clarifying definition and a commonly convincing justification in favour of that special kind of religion.[29]

In the new era: a close relationship between monotheism and the new natural sciences

'Religion and science' – it all depends on how the terms are perceived. We have already commented on the term 'science', and in the previous paragraph, we have pointed to the pluralism of 'religions'. Now, to get started, let us focus on some main points in the interplay between science and religion in Western history.

i During the medieval ages in Western Europe, there was a close relationship between theology and philosophy (in many ways the main sciences at the time), and there was certainly an intimate relationship between theology and religion, be it Jewish, Christian, or Islamic. In Platonic (neo-Platonic) and Aristotelian philosophy, there were major theological elements, both in ontology and epistemology and in moral and political theory.

ii From the late Medieval Age into the new era, up to the eighteenth century, there was similarly a close relationship between monotheistic theology and religion on the one hand, and the emerging new natural sciences on the other.[30] In this connection, there were two underlying narratives: (a) The narrative of the Two Books: there were the Holy Scriptures, written by God and to be interpreted by the theologians, and the Book of Nature, written by God in mathematical symbols, to be discovered and reformulated, in a mathematical language, by the natural scientists. (b) The narrative of God as Mechanical Mastermind: the universe,[31] as a gigantic mechanical clockwork, has God as its mechanical mastermind, and by their experimental work, it is up to the natural scientists to discover the underlying laws of nature and formulate them in a mathematical language.

---

29 Those who question this may ask themselves whether they think that witchcraft or satanism (new or old) and New Age in various shapes deserve extraordinary respect and legal protection.

30 See Steven Shapin, *The Scientific Revolution*, University of Chicago Press, Chicago 1996.

31 Cf., e.g., Gilje, Nils, and Gunnar Skirbekk. *A History of Western Thought: from Ancient Greece to the twentieth century*. Routledge, London and New York 2001, chapter 7 and 9 on the mechanical worldview.

14 Science and religion

This certainly went against some of the main ideas in the Aristotelian philosophy of nature, and thus it went counter to those theologians who insisted on the Aristotelian perspective. The trial against Galileo Galilei in 1633 is the paradigmatic case of this controversy. However, in spite of this controversy, the new natural scientists in Western Europe worked against the background of religious images. Atheism was largely a French invention by the end of the eighteenth century! Even a critical enlightenment philosopher like Voltaire was a deist.

My second point on religion and sciences is as follows: at the outset, in the new era, there was in many ways a close and positive relationship between religion and science, not least among the new natural scientists.

The inherent need for a critique of religion

Earlier, we referred to the need for a self-critical critique of the sciences (*Wissenschaftskritik*). This includes theology and philosophy. However, there is also a need for an informed and self-critical critique of religion (as we already indicated earlier). But there are different (partly overlapping) kinds of critique of religion, in short:

Moral-based criticism of religion argues that certain forms of religion are morally problematic or reprehensible. The targets are utterances and demands found in religious scriptures or doctrines but also acts and attitudes ascribed to religious persons and institutions.

External criticism of religion holds that certain forms of religion are merely epiphenomena, expressions of underlying psychological and social circumstances (e.g. Freud and Marx).

Internal criticism of religion takes religious utterances literally and thereby raises an intellectual criticism of the level of precision and of the truth-claims in that which is uttered or presupposed. By extension (and related to psychologizing interpretations), we find religious criticism in the shape of *deconstruction*, as in Nietzsche.

The role of the various sciences, for the critique of religion, could be summarized as follows:

i *External, causal explanation*: referring to social causes, such as in Karl Marx – religion as "opium for the people", and thus as "false consciousness" – or psychological and psychiatric causes, as in Freud (religion as psychological displacement).[32]

---

32 But then again, we have sociological pro-arguments in favour of religion, such as in Émile Durkheim and Jürgen Habermas, who see religion as important for social cohesion.

ii *Historical positivism*: as the secularization thesis, e.g. in Auguste Comte – who saw history as a development in different stages: the religious, metaphysical, and scientific stages.[33]

iii *Natural scientific knowledge*: e.g. the dramatic history of the origin of the earth and of the evolution of species, or about everyday life and political events, where an appeal to magical forces, or to commands, or prohibitions from divine powers are no longer seen as credible.

iv *Historic-philological textual critique*: those religions that are based on Holy Scriptures cannot avoid comparative and contextualizing interpretations and textual analyses.

v *Logical positivism*: a theory of *knowledge* and *language*, focusing on the question as to which utterances can be seen as cognitively meaningful, and giving the following answer: only well-formed, empirically verifiable propositions are cognitively meaningful! Hence, the religious language is, just as normative statements, void of cognitive meaning.[34]

In short, talking about the relationship between religion and science, these critical arguments should be mentioned. However, these are the kinds of arguments, well-known in modern societies, that have been seriously considered by contemporary theologians, and for this reason, modern university-based theology has been intellectually modernized and updated.[35] Here again, there were long learning processes. We may briefly recall some major points: For example, when Western Europe saw the formation of new states and Protestantism emerged in various forms, there was also a renewed concern for *interpreting* disciplines: the interpretation of *legal* texts in jurisprudence and the interpretation of *religious* texts in theology. For a text does not interpret itself; it has to be interpreted by somebody. Moreover, there are often different interpretations of the same text. Hence, we are faced with the question: Why is *my* interpretation better than the other interpretations? For a serious answer to this question, one has to give *reasons* as to why one interpretation is more precise, more reliable, and trustworthy than another. Moreover, different religions have *different* Holy Scriptures, and hence we are faced with the question: Why are my texts the right ones and not those of the

---

33 But then there are counterarguments, e.g. in late Habermas, who rejects the secularization thesis and emphasizes religion as a resource of insight and values needed in modern societies. Cf. *Zwischen Naturalismus und Religion*, Suhrkamp, Frankfurt a.M. 2005, English translation: *Between Naturalism and Religion*. Wiley. 2014, and *Auch eine Geschichte der Philosophie*, Suhrkamp, Berlin 2019. Cf. the discussion of Habermas, chapter 6, below.

34 Void of meaning cognitively, but not emotionally! Cf. Alfred Ayer and the Vienna School.

35 This applies to philosophy of religion and rational (non-credal) theology, see two contributions from (theistic) philosophy of religion: Peter Rohs, *Der Platz zum Glauben*, Mentis Verlag, Münster 2013, and Holm Tetens, *Gott denken. Ein Versuch über rationale Theologie*, Reclam, Stuttgart 2015.

16 Science and religion

others? In short, there is an inherent need, within the religions based on Holy Scriptures, to move from interpretation towards rational argumentation.

This reminds us of Enlightenment, as in Kant's famous definition: *sapere aude!* Have the courage to use your own reason! – with the addition: in a self-critical discussion with other reasonable people! Moreover, in Kant, the term 'critique' does not mean a negative denial, but a serious test, aiming to improve.[36]

Hence, modern societies are science-based, not only by the new natural sciences but also by renewed interpretive disciplines and self-critical argumentation.

However, this has not been recognized and acknowledged by everybody. For instance, Sayyid Qutb[37] (1906–1966) was in favour of natural sciences, and certainly of his own religious convictions, but he disliked the humanities and social sciences. In this sense, he was *semi-modern*. The same is true of people like Mahmoud Ahmadinejad, engineer and religious fundamentalist (president of Iran 2005–2013), and also of influential groups in the United States who tend to embrace the natural sciences,[38] but not the Enlightenment tradition.[39]

This is my third point: For all three monotheistic religions, there is an *inherent need* for a *critique of religion*. (Critique is understood as purging, not as rejection.) However, due to the critical interplay between the various sciences and religion, modern university-based theology in the Western world has largely been intellectually informed and updated.

Modernization of consciousness

But is not religion (whatever it may mean) beyond the scope of rationality, either because it is deeply personal or because it can only be understood in an internal perspective, that is, by the believers themselves,[40] but not by and for the non-religious, i.e. not from an external point of view?

There is something to be said for such objections. On the other hand, when it comes to the three monotheistic religions – Judaism, Christianity, and Islam – they do raise universal validity-claims, each one of them, about their Holy Scriptures and about their own conception of the one and only God. Structurally, on these decisive points, the three monotheistic religions are faced with the *same kind* of challenges, and consequently, due to these universal validity-claims, they are inherently open to enlightenment and rational criticism (as purging).

---

36 Cf. Kant's book titles, such as 'critique' of pure reason and of practical reason.
37 Sayyid Qutb was one of the leading ideologists in the Muslim Brotherhood, cf. his book *Milestones*, Islamic Book Service, New Delhi 1998 (original 1964).
38 In short: from Francis Bacon and Isaac Newton. But not so much Charles Darwin.
39 In short, from Voltaire and Hume.
40 Or perhaps more safely by their spokespersons, such as rabbis, priests, or imams!

Eight points about science and religion **17**

We recall the two fundamental traits that these three monotheistic religions have in common: (i) They are, all three of them, *based on Holy Scriptures*. And in a modern pluralistic society, we are faced with the fact that there are *other interpretations* of "my" Holy Scriptures. Hence the question: Why are my interpretations the right ones? And we must acknowledge that there are other people who have *other Holy Scriptures*. Hence the question: Why are my texts the right ones? To answer these questions, reflexivity and reasoning are needed. Self-critical interpretations and reasonable argumentations are required. (ii) For all three monotheistic religions, there is only one God, who is at the same time benevolent and almighty (in one way or the other), and thus they are, all three, *inter alia* confronted with *the problem of evil*, in one way or another, as a theological challenge, in need of serious reflection and argumentation.[41]

At the same time, there are, of course, *a range of differences* between (and within) these three world religions. They are, already from the outset, quite dissimilar due to different historical conditions and socio-political preconditions, e.g. as to whether they operated inside or outside the realm of political and military power,[42] or as to how they were interrelated to the institutional and epistemic developments that formed parts of early modernization processes.

But all three are today faced with the same basic needs for epistemic and institutional *adaptation* to the positive and necessary demands for an enlightened modernity, in short, for a "modernization of consciousness"[43]:

a A recognition of various kinds of insight and knowledge that are established in a responsible and self-critical way by various sciences and scholarly disciplines – critically conceived, but still the best we have. Religious teaching and practices should be adapted accordingly.

b A self-critical reflection on, and recognition of, the pluralism of religions and other "comprehensive doctrines."[44] Religious teaching and practices should be adapted accordingly.

c Acknowledgement of the differentiation in modern societies between various institutions and their inherent roles, for instance, the distinction between roles in private life and roles in professional life or in public positions, including the difference between the legal system and religion. Religious teaching and practices should be adapted accordingly.

41 We will get back to the problem of evil in the next chapter.

42 Cf. Ahmet Kuru, on this issue, particularly with regard to Islam – see later chapters in the present collection.

43 "Modernisierung des (religiösen) Bewusstseins" [modernization of (religious) consciousness], cf. Jürgen Habermas, *Zwischen Naturalismus und Religion*, Suhrkamp, Frankfurt a.M. 2005, s. 146. English translation Habermas, *Between Naturalism and Religion*. 1st edn. Wiley. 2014. Chapter 8, "The Boundary between Faith and Knowledge: On the Reception and Contemporary Importance of Kant's Philosophy of Religion" under point (11).

44 "Comprehensive Doctrines", John Rawls, *Political Liberalism*, Columbia University Press, New York 1993, e.g. p. 58.

18 Science and religion

When these demands for a "modernization of consciousness" are *not* dealt with appropriately, then we do not live up to basic preconditions for modern societies, with a variety of sciences and scholarly disciplines, and with institutional differentiations and their inherent roles.

Earlier, we focused on the need for a self-critical critique of the sciences. Now we have focused on a need for a self-critical critique of religion, in its interplay with the sciences in modern societies. It is worth recalling that critique in this connection does not mean rejection. The term should be taken in its Kantian sense: critique as a clarifying (and formative) process.[45] The point of the critique in this sense is not a negative act of rejection, but a constructive act of improvement.[46]

As my fourth and final point, I would therefore rearticulate my main message on science and religion in modern societies: "Religion" is no longer a precise term, and it is no longer self-evident that everything that is denoted "religion" should be respected and legally supported. In order to warrant respect and legal support, normative justification is required in each case.

In short, religion is currently a legitimate part of the modern world, though not without a critical interplay with the various sciences, which implies both a self-critical critique of the sciences and a self-critical and purifying critique of religion, the latter characterized by what some people refer to as a 'modernization of consciousness'. Briefly stated, these are my concluding remarks on science and religion in a modern world.

45 Again, as it is used in the Kantian 'critique of pure reason' and 'critique of practical reason'. E.g. 'durch Kritik geläutert[]', ('clarified by criticism'), in preface, 2nd edn. (Vorrede zur zweiten Auflage), *Kritik der reinen Vernunft*, Felix Meiner Verlag, Würzburg 1956, p. 24.

46 But such purging does not leave things in their original state: Prominent interpretations of text and tradition and of credal dogma must be tested and reconciled, cf., e.g., Peter Rohs, *Der Platz zum Glauben*, Mentis Verlag, Münster 2013.

2

TO SPEAK OF GOD IN THE LIGHT OF THE PROBLEM OF EVIL

On the need for theology and the danger of unintended blasphemy[1]

Background

Once again, religion is subject to public debate, often in relation to issues of immigration and integration. But 'the return of religion' holds a broader relevance. It does not only refer to the traditional monotheistic religions (Judaism, Christianity, and Islam), but also to new religious movements, from New Age to scientology and satanism, as well as other world religions, such as Hinduism and Buddhism, not to mention a range of popular and traditional conceptions of good and evil forces. The word 'religion' is therefore ambiguous; it can no longer be used without clarification.

But if we stick to the three monotheistic religions, we can make the following observations: They all operate with the conception that there is one God, and they all operate with certain validity claims. Hence theology is required, as a reasonable clarification of the various validity claims as to how we can and should relate to God, and of how we should live our lives.

With the return of religion, we are therefore, *inter alia*, faced with a need for a renewed theologian discussion. However, theologian perspectives have largely been absent from the public debate. That is regrettable since theologian discussion may be enlightening, not the least when it comes to the question of 'the problem of evil', which inevitably manifests itself in all three monotheistic religions.

---

1 Previously published in Gunnar Skirbekk, *Krise og medansvar*, Res Publica, Oslo 2016. Slightly revised.

DOI: 10.4324/9781003441618-3

20 Science and religion

Without such clarifications, it may well happen that those who see them-selves as God-fearing, true believers actually appear as blasphemous, by unintentionally representing God as a brutish or ridiculous figure.

The problem

The problem of evil is well-known: If God is benevolent, almighty, and omniscient, then how can evil exist in the world? In the case that God does not *want* to prevent evil, then how can he be benevolent? In the case that God *cannot* prevent evil, then how can he be almighty? In the case that God doesn't *know* about everything and everyone, then how can he be omnisci-ent? In other words, if God is benevolent, almighty, and omniscient, how can there be evil?

These questions have been pondered by many people; throughout time, the problem of evil has been approached from different perspectives and in different ways, from the Book of Job, through stoicism, neo-Platonism, and Manichaeism to Augustine and Thomas Aquinas, and further on. In the early eighteenth century, Leibniz provided a philosophical defence in his work *Théodicée*,[2] where he wants to show that God has chosen the best of all possible universes. That which, for us, appears as evil, should be seen in this overarching perspective: We live in the best of all possible worlds.

Leibniz had discussed this problem with the electress Sophia Charlotte (1668–1705). The electress, as a thought experiment, suggested avoiding the problem of evil by separating between faith and reason in such matters. Against this position, Leibniz, as a philosophical rationalist, emphasized that there is a rational answer to this problem. But in 1755, sometime after Leibniz had published his defence, *Théodicée* (in 1710), Lisbon was struck by an earthquake, with great fires and tsunamis, which resulted in extensive mate-rial damage and an immense number of deaths. This was, in all respects, a shocking event. How could this happen in the best of all possible worlds? What good could come of such a tragedy? Would it not, from all reasonable perspectives, be better if this had never occurred?

Not long after this, in 1759, Voltaire published his caustic satire *Candide ou l'Optimisme*, which exposed the Leibnizian optimism to public disgrace.

Around the same time, Kant was pondering the problem of evil, as a phi-losopher of the Enlightenment and protestant. But he finally concluded that philosophy is unable to provide an answer.[3] Kant distinguishes between

---

2 The word *théodicée* was first coined by Leibniz in 1696 as a compound of two Greek words: God and justice. Full title: *Essais de théodicée sur la bonté de Dieu, la liberté de l'homme et l'origine du mal*. Published in 1710, by Isaac Troyel in Amsterdam.

3 In 1791, Kant speaks of the failure of all philosophical attempts to solve the dilemma [«Das Misslingen aller philosophischen Versuche in der Theodicee», Akad.-A. 8, 255].

To speak of God in light of the problem of evil **21**

knowledge, morality, and faith, between questions about what we can know, what we should do, and what we dare to hope for. The normative appears as duty-ethics based on the individual and as a future-oriented aim towards a universal rule of law for all. In this way, 'the practical' is separated from the theoretical as well as from the religious.

In Hegel, 'reconciliation' is an inherent aspect of societal development in the form of a (future) goal. But for all the previous generations, who have experienced the problem of evil as a brutal reality, this is not very satisfactory. How should all the tragedies and shattered lives possibly be justified and 'reconciled' on the basis of a future utopia? Similar objections could be raised against a Marxist optimism of the future, not the least when the rulers actively and deliberately sacrifice contemporary generations for an idea of a future and earthly harmony.

Here, as in the Christian theodicy, the price may appear as far too high and exceedingly unreasonable. True enough, a lot of evils may be interpreted and explained in a way which makes reconciliation possible. But when the world's evils appear as massive and meaningless, such as the earthquake in Lisbon, and as in Auschwitz, the challenges become existential as well as intellectual. Where was the voice of God in Auschwitz? A shattering question for Jews who believe in God's guiding hand in history. What kind of future harmony or peace should ever be able to explain and justify what happened there?

For Mosaic Jews, but also for other Abrahamic monotheists, Auschwitz constitutes an existential and intellectual challenge. God, has he forsaken us?

Can we write poetry after Auschwitz?[4] And what could a theodicy look like after Auschwitz? Hans Jonas, a Jewish intellectual, gets straight to the point with his text "The Concept of God after Auschwitz: A Jewish Voice" (*Der Gottesbegriff nach Auschwitz. Eine jüdische Stimme*).[5]

Notwithstanding, the discussions persist,[6] even after Auschwitz and Hiroshima, after Uganda, after Srebrenica, after Darfur and Gaza, after Haiti, and the discussion continues as we are now faced with the potentiality of exceedingly grim future scenarios. What does it mean, in this day and age, to speak of God in the light of the problem of evil?

---

4 Cf. Theodor Adorno.
5 Published by Suhrkamp Taschenbuch, Fr.a.M. 1987. English ref: Jonas, Hans. The Concept of God after Auschwitz: A Jewish Voice. *The Journal of Religion*, 67(1): 1987, pp. 1–13. JSTOR, http://www.jstor.org/stable/1203313. Accessed 17 August 2022. The Norwegian public debate has primarily revolved around the doctrine of Hell, i.e. the evil of the afterlife, rather than the evil in the world (cf. the discussion between Ole Hallesby and bishop Schjelderup). In this sense, my contribution in the book *Nihilism?* (English version 1972) can be regarded as an exception.
6 Cf. Atle Ottesen Søvik, *The Problem of Evil and the Power of God. On the Coherence and Authenticity of Some Christian Theodicies with Different Understanding of God's Power*, doctoral dissertation, MF Norwegian School of Theology, Religion and Society, 2009.

22 Science and religion

This is not a matter of whether or not God exists, but of how to speak of and conceive of God in the light of the problem of evil. It is a matter of mutual interpretation, between the conception of God on the one hand and the problem of evil on the other: The problem of evil will differ with different interpretations of the conceptions of God, and likewise, the conception of God will have to be adjusted with the various interpretations of the problem of evil.

I am no theologian, nor am I an expert in religious history or sociology. My discipline is philosophy, but in this chapter, I will leave professional philosophy behind and feel my way as a questioning and fallible person. My reasoning is tentative, as is appropriate for the essay genre. And I will paint with a broad brush, steering clear of many of the specifications and reservations that the topic invites. The text will be structured as follows:

1 Shifts over time in the relationship between faith in God and the perception of a religious justification of morality
2 Notes on the three monotheistic religions concerning the conception of God and the way they were influenced by different socio-historical contexts
3 The problem of evil in the light of different conceptions of God, in the three monotheistic religions
4 What implications does this have for speaking of God?
5 What implications does this have for the perception of the Holy?

Shifts over time in the relationship between faith in God and the perception of a religious justification of morality

In the 1950s, in our corner of the world, religious faith was under negative intellectual pressure, from positivism and cultural radicalism.[7] But it was a widespread notion that religion (conventional Norwegian Christianity) is able to justify moral doctrines and principles, as opposed to positivism, which refrains from giving a normative justification of morality.

At the same time, religious faith focused on Jesus Christ and Bible history rather than theology, or on ecstatic contact with the Divine (as in the charismatic Pentecostal movement). In other words, the focus was on the Son and The Holy Spirit, two of the three parts of the Holy Trinity, rather than the Father (to stay true to the terminology), and in both cases, the personal experience played a more important part than did intellectual labour and insight – in short, psychology (and pedagogy) rather than theology.

Today, we see a revitalization of religion in Norway and internationally. Positivism has been defeated. Currently, it is far more acceptable to be

---

7 Mainly by literati, often inspired by Freud.

religious, to believe in God. At the same time, religion has become more pluralistic, both as a social fact and as a conceptual approach (but what is religion, really? – this question no longer has a clear and unequivocal answer[8]). What is more, we see bestiality in the name of religion, often carried out by means of modern technology and weapons. Therefore, it is currently harder to imagine "religion" (without clarification) as an antidote to bestiality or as a justification for universal morality. In this sense a shift has occurred in the relationship between faith and morality: more room for faith, less room for religion as basis for universal morality.

The theological discussions are extensive, but in our modern societies, faith in God is often perceived in terms of a vague personal experience of "something greater than me", without a clear theological profile. Or faith in God may take the shape of premodern and unenlightened fundamentalism, whether it is in the United States, in Israel, or in the Middle East (in all of the three monotheistic religions).

Notes on the three monotheistic religions concerning the conception of God and the way they were influenced by different socio-historical contexts

Here we operate with three monotheistic religions, Judaism, Christianity, Islam. There is, of course, significant variations between these three when it comes to the conception of God. We here remain with these three, in simple ideal-type versions, and our account will be brief and tentative:

Judaism is at the outset a tribal religion. God appears as a superior actor in the history of the Jews,[9] as it is written in the Jewish Holy Scriptures.[10]

The later socio-historical context is shaped by diaspora, which generates a multitude of local Jewish communities, dispersed over a range of different countries and cultures, where they in different ways maintain Jewish traditions and literary culture, which often generate a certain ambiguity, characteristic for people who are integrated in a general community, but who at the same time maintain an alternative perspective. A remarkable number of scientists and intellectuals are of Jewish descent.

In *Christianity*, God appears, first and foremost, through Jesus Christ, as a revelation in history, through Jesus' life, suffering, and death, transmitted through

---

8 As mentioned in the introduction: "Religion" may refer to a lot of things, from the three monotheistic religions and variations within them, to world religions such as Hinduism and Buddhism, onwards to all kinds of new religions, including scientology and satanism, not to mention witchcraft and animism. When we (with Habermas) talk about religion in this context, we are thus referring to specific religions and, what is more, to modern versions of these religions.

9 A God who intervenes in the history of all populations (cf. the flood in Genesis) but who has the Jews as his chosen people.

10 Cf. what is referred to as the Old Testament in the Christian tradition.

24 Science and religion

Holy Scriptures and through the Christian tradition. Christianity is universal. It applies to all. "There is neither Jew nor Greek, [] there is neither male nor female."[11]

At the outset, the socio-historical context is a matter of being in opposition to the powerful, be it Jewish or Roman rule. Moreover, Christians have a particular concern for the weak. In time, Christianity becomes a part of the political establishment, but with an institutional tension between State and Church, ideologically and theologically between the Sovereign and God, politically between secular and clerical actors and institutions. This opens up a space for freedom which is not present when political and religious power overlap without such differentiations.

In *Islam*, God appears through the Qur'an, but also through the Prophet's life and teachings in other Holy Scriptures (*Hadith*), transmitted through different interpretative traditions.[12] Islam is universal. It applies to all. As a book granted by God, the Qur'an, with supplements from other Holy Scriptures,[13] claims the authority to provide universal answers to how we should lead and organize our lives.

The socio-cultural context quickly became such that Islam gained a political (and military) position. Hence, there was a low degree of institutional differentiation between the political and the religious domains.[14] This also left little room for the kind of education where one learns to see and understand oneself from the outside and where one has to defend oneself against those in power. In short, not due to inherent theologian preconditions[15]

---

11 Galatians, 3.28.
12 Cf. Sunni and Shia, and different popular traditions.
13 Cf. Sharia based in the Qur'an and Hadith and the interpretative traditions.
14 Cf. corresponding points made by Ahmet Kuru, discussed in Part IV in this collection. Cf. the contrast to Christianity, which until the end of the 400s A.D. lived in opposition, before Christianity became an official religion (just before the fall of the Roman Empire), and from that point on, two institutions developed – Church and State – which remained for several hundred years (through the Medieval Age). This paves the ground for Gelasius' doctrine of the two powers (ca. 400 A.D.), a doctrine which is maintained throughout the Medieval Age. In the 1000s, the battle intensifies in the nomination of bishops, the Investiture Controversy, which continues for a couple of hundred years, and which ended with a strengthened position on behalf of the papacy (in the 1200s). This is, in short, the period from Augustine to Thomas Aquinas. In the late Medieval Ages (with theorists such as Marsilius and Ockham), the theologian justification for the pope's politico-institutional power was challenged. In the wake of this, we get the Reformation and the national monarchies, which subjects the Church (or churches) to State rule (from Henry VIII in England to Luther and the Protestant sovereigns in Germany and North-Western Europe).
15 The word-for-word formulations in the different Holy Scriptures is one thing (this applies to all of the three monotheistic religions, cf. e.g. Surah 8, verse 12 f. in the Qur'an). The theologian interpretation is another matter. In the latter case, there is a crucial difference between contexts where those who hold interpretative authority are educated and socialised into an informed and enlightened university community (as has become the case in North-Western Europe), or if priests and religious leaders are shaped in intellectually closed environments, whether it is organized by Christian sects in North America, in Qur'an schools in the Muslim communities, or in Talmud schools in Israel.

but due to the socio-historical context, Islam has to a lesser extent than Judaism and Christianity had the opportunity to develop an ability of self-reflecting intellectual critique.[16]

Seen from the Middle Kingdom (i.e. China), we could here speak of three Western monotheistic religions, where Judaism is the oldest and Islam is the youngest.

The problem of evil in the light of different conceptions of God in the three monotheistic religions

Judaism's notion of Jews as 'God's chosen people' might appear bizarre after Auschwitz and the Holocaust. This is the problem of evil 'head on'.

Nevertheless, Judaism, as a tradition and historical tribal religion, is fairly robust, for those who are part of the tribe.[17]

Moreover, there are several reflected Jewish intellectuals who interpret and relativize the idea of God's almighty presence.[18]

Christianity, with the doctrine of the Trinity where God is three *personae* (three ways of showing himself), may seem confusing and theologically complicated: God is a small child who, when he becomes an adult, is tortured and nailed to a cross, while God is at the same time the almighty creator, the one who provides the rules for everything and everyone, and who judges everyone, the living and the dead, in accordance with these rules, and then enforces these judgements, potentially by way of eternal damnation in Hell, while at the same time manifesting himself as the Holy Spirit. When God is conceived as creator, legislator, judge, and enforcer,[19] we immediately find ourselves faced with the problem of evil.

But then again, there is – precisely through the Trinity, with the life and Passion of the Christ – a strong focus on vulnerable lives and compassion for the unfortunate. (All of the three Christian holidays remind us of this: Christmas, Easter, Pentecost – vulnerable infant, suffering and death, spiritual unanimity – vulnerable soul, body, and unanimity.) In this sense, there are, in the narrative, in the stories about the life of Christ in the New Testament, clearly cues that create a tension in the teachings about God as almighty (at least if this is understood in a straightforward sense.)

16 Of course, such learning processes are not consistently present in Christianity and Judaism either (North American evangelicals and Israeli occupants are unfortunate examples.) Yet, and again, cf. Ahmet Kuru later in this collection.

17 After World War II, many Jews found themselves unable to believe in Jahve, but still they maintained their Jewish identity.

18 From Spinoza and Mendelsohn through Marx and Freud to Marcuse and Bloch, Hans Jonas and Aron Cicourel.

19 Cf. The Apostle's Creed Recitation "I believe in God, the Father Almighty, maker of heaven and earth … [and who] will come to judge the living and the dead." ("Credo in Deum, Patrem omnipotentem, Creatorem caeli et terrae, … inde venturus est iudicare vivos et mortuos.")

26 Science and religion

Islam is neither a tribal religion nor a Trinity religion. At first glance, this may look like an advantage: one God, Muhammed is his Prophet, and the teachings apply to all populations. In many ways, this is the most clear-cut monotheism of them all: One God has created (and maintains) everything that exists; he provides the rules; he judges all (to Hell or to Paradise), and he enforces the judgements.

This may seem tantalizingly simple.[20] But the price for this clear-cut conception of God, for this straightforward theology, is a radicalization of the problem of evil. Here, there are no hints about a vulnerable God. For it is precisely in such a monotheism, where one almighty God at the same time is creator, legislator, judge, and enforcer that the problem of evil becomes particularly pressing.

What implications does this have for speaking of God?

The problem of evil is not an argument against (or for) the existence of God. But this problem influences the way in which we can speak and think about God. It is decisive for the conception of God. (Just as different interpretations of the God concept provide different versions of the problem of evil. Here hermeneutics goes both ways.)

Extending the problem of evil, the question emerges of how we should interpret and understand that which is written in the Holy Scriptures, particularly about what God (according to these scriptures and tradition-based interpretations) appears to command or prohibit. We will touch upon what this may mean below, but first, a more general comment.

Based in (i) the notion of God as creator, legislator, judge, and enforcer, and based in (ii) the contents of different Holy Scriptures (The Old and the New Testament, the Qur'an, and other Holy Scriptures) and which is interpreted from different traditional perspectives, there appears to be, as far as I can see, three interpretational ideal types for the concept of God, intellectually speaking:

---

20 On the view of Islam theology as simple and therefore attractive, cf. Diego Gambetta and Steffen Hertog, "Engineers of Jihad", in Sociology Working Papers, 2007–2010, University of Oxford, e.g. footnote 52, see www.nuff.ox.ac.uk/users/gambetta/Engineers%20of%20Jihad.pdf. This empirically based argument furthermore shows a correlation between the thinking of engineers and authoritarian (violent) Islamism; in short, a warped semi-modernization (focusing on instrumental rationality and authoritarian measures, as opposed to critical-argumentative rationality and democratic approaches). In this context, cf. the attempt of Islamists to distinguish between (i) instrumental natural sciences and technology which are taken to be in harmony with Islam and (ii) research in social sciences and the humanities which include historical and philological textual critique, and which are rejected (as in Sayyid Qutb, 1906–1966; cf. *Milestones*, New Delhi, Islamic Book Service 1998 (original 1964)). For critical remarks on the first point, cf. Turkish-American physicist E. Taner, *An Illusion of Harmony. Science and Religion in Islam*, Prometheus Books, Amherst, NY 2007.

God appears as tyrannical.

God appears as foolish.

God does not seem to have a clear relevance for all our choices of actions.[21]

With a notion of God as the creator of everything and everyone, as simultaneously legislator and judge, and on top of that as the enforcer who punishes the living as well as the dead (potentially by way of Hell and eternal damnation), God immediately appears as a tyrant. In a clear-cut monotheism of this kind, we face the problem of evil 'head on', and thus we get the attempts to come up with a *theodicy*.

Included here is, e.g., the extensive debate on whether humans can be said to have free will, freedom to choose evil, and also whether much of that which appears as evil to us (such as plagues and famines) is actually God's righteous punishment for the evil choices that man himself has made. But this leads us directly to the question of what it means, if this is the case, that God is almighty and omniscient, by virtue of being the creator of everything and everyone and being the one that at all times knows all about everything and everyone. In short (as a reminder): Even if we as humans indeed had free will, then it is because God wanted it so, made it so, and knew what it would lead to, and, moreover, provided the rules that the sinful will be judged by.[22]

True enough, some of that which in a narrow perspective appears as evil (e.g. an accident), may from a broader perspective turn out to be meaningful (because we learned something from it). And much of that which appears as evil (e.g. that life is finite), will upon closer inspection appear as necessary.[23] In addition come the aforementioned arguments about God's righteous punishment for the acts that humans have committed in this life, or as a legitimate warning to weak souls to make them refrain from evil acts in the future. But faced with *extensive* natural disasters (such as the earthquake in Lisbon) or *incomprehensible* misdeeds (such as Auschwitz and Holocaust), these arguments are unconvincing: There is no superior perspective from which such tragedies may be reconciled and turned into something good! Neither is it true that tragedies of this kind appear as necessary in a philosophical sense. Nor can natural disasters like the earthquake in Lisbon be perceived as self-inflicted. And if this were to be taken as God's collective punishment for human sin, that is indeed a good reason to take a critical approach towards the monotheistic conception of God, of God as almighty and omnipotent, creator of everything and everyone.

---

21 But if God, based in these scriptures, does not appear as having a clear relevance for all our choices of action, a religious perspective on life and the world may still have a range of implications for different attitudes and directions, e.g. an awe for vulnerable life, cf. Hans Jonas and Albert Schweitzer.

22 Without differentiating between legislative, judicial, and executive power; God is the sole ruler in all of these domains, as an autocratic sovereign.

23 This resonates with Leibniz' argument.

28 Science and religion

In short, *moderate* evil can be tackled, but *radical* and *extensive* evil requires other approaches.

We will not go into that debate here. We will let it suffice to say that without some kind of modification of the blunt interpretation of a monotheistic conception of God, it is hard to make sense of it, intellectually speaking.[24]

So, might one then turn it around and see this dilemma as springing from the problem that human reason is simply unable to understand God (or God's essence, as one used to say): One's relationship to God is a matter of *faith*, not of reason![25] But then we approach a third alternative, which we touched upon earlier: For our human understanding, God is a mystery. In this sense, any talk of God must necessarily be tentative. For our human thought, God is distant. This is a way out of the theological dilemma of the problem of evil. But if we go down this road, it is necessary to adjust our conceptualizations as well as the rhetoric.

Beyond the writings that hold direct relevance for the problem of evil, the Holy Scriptures contain many rules concerning how we should lead our lives, supported by traditional interpretations. Some of these rules are often understood as more or less direct representations of the will of God, and his commandments, which in turn leads us to the question of how the will of God, and therefore God's essence, can and should be conceived.

Let us start off with the terminology by taking a closer look at the notion of Paradise, with its eternal bliss, as opposed to Hell with eternal torment. The notion of Hell is morally challenging; there is a striking lack of proportionality between the offence and the punishment. But the notion of Hell is also conceptually challenging – for example, if the punishment is eternal pain on a physical level, we get the impression that Hell is a physical space, a notion which poses further intellectual problems. The notion of Paradise is likewise problematic. It is not made easier if some in addition think that martyrs (as a reward for glorious deeds) will meet virgins in Paradise.[26] Apart from the normative issues of such a notion: how is this to be conceived?[27]

---

24 Here, again, Hans Jonas is relevant, with his novel take on the conception of omnipotence, focusing on a compassionate God and on man's co-responsibility.

25 This brings us deep into theology, e.g. with Luther (as a nominalist) who separates between the use of reason in mundane matters and faith (through grace) in religious matters, or Thomas Aquinas who (with his conceptual realism) operates with reason-based arguments for the existence of God, but not for God's essence, which is, for Thomas as well, solely available through the revelation, correctly understood.

26 Cf., e.g., "How Many Wives Will the Believer Have in Paradise?" (www.livingislam.org/fiqhi/sp2-gfh_e.html#9) by Shaykh Gibril Haddad (cf. e.g. Zayd ibn Arqam, 2a: "[E]ach of them will be given the strength of a hundred men in his eating, drinking, coitus and pleasures").

27 One strategy has been to claim that God/Allah/Jahve is a mystery to us, while at the same time claiming that what is stated in the Holy Scriptures is to be taken literally. But that does not make sense: If we are to understand these scriptures as the word of God in any literal sense, then God frequently appears as tyrannical or foolish, rather than as a mystery.

What does it mean to be a virgin in Paradise? It is reasonable to assume that a virgin is a woman with certain physical attributes. If so, we are talking about spatial phenomena – but where? And do these notions mean that men are equally endowed? (Do men get erections in Paradise? Do they have intercourse with these virgins? If so, where does it take place – out in the open for all to see, or are there secluded areas for such practices?) In short, the more we think about it, the more puzzling it becomes, i.e., the more unreasonable it becomes. I do not state this with the intention to mock or provoke but in an attempt to illustrate a conceptual point: To make Paradise relevant to our mundane lives is a hazardous endeavour. The result tends to become conceptually unreasonable. Therefore, it is reasonable to interpret such statements allegorically, as is the norm in modern theology. But that, in turn, implies that religion is modernized and tempered.

The Holy Scriptures contain rules that are relevant (or that many hold to be relevant) for how we should lead our lives. They concern our relationship to our neighbour, our relationship to the Sacred, and to ourselves. But in addition to this, there are many (in all of the three monotheistic religions, partly based in Holy Scriptures and partly based in specific traditions) who hold that it is religiously required not only that we *behave* in certain ways but also that we *dress* in certain ways and that we *eat* and *drink* in certain ways, and not otherwise. For instance, many take a negative stance towards eating pork. The pig is seen as an impure animal. Therefore, visual representations of pigs in public spaces (such as "the three little pigs" in hospitals and in nursery schools) may be seen as reprehensible, from a religious perspective. Three comments on this:

i   *The problem of pluralism*: While a large number of people look with distaste at the pig and find it offensive that pigs are portrayed and mentioned in a positive way, there are a great many people, e.g. the Chinese, who view the pig as a symbol of good fortune.[28] The point is this: Because there is a vast range of different, often contradictory, "religious" (and "secular") opinions about what the public space should look like, it is in practice difficult, and often *logically impossible*, to please everyone. The problem intensifies with the number of different parties involved. For instance, regarding the question of whether Christians and Muslims, respectively, can accept both calls to worship and church bells, there is also a third party involved who wants peace and quiet and who will have none of what they experience as religious noise in the public space.[29]

---

28 These are vast numbers, each group approaching 1.3 billion (if we count Muslims and Jews in the one group and the Chinese in the other), so it is a bit tricky to talk about minorities in this context.
29 And maybe there are satanists who (based in their religious conviction) would want blasphemous exclamations to resonate through the public space, etc.

30 Science and religion

ii   *Socio-historical explanations*: Negative attitudes towards pigs and pork are understandable in societies where pigs (and dogs) are associated with scabby creatures who ramble around in rubbish dumps and open sewage (cf. the danger of trichina in pork). But this is not the case for modern hygienic pig farming (nor was it the case for the wild boars in Gaul). In modern societies, the prohibition of pork appears unfounded, rationally speaking – but at the same time as socio-historically understandable.[30] It is also understandable psychologically speaking: Just as most people are appalled by the idea of eating rat meat, some may have been trained to have corresponding emotions towards eating pig; at a psychological level, we take no issue with this. But it becomes problematic if this is explained as God's will and command, that *this* is the reason why we should show an extraordinary respect for such emotions.[31]

iii   *The problem of blasphemy*: But then, some will claim that "this is just how it is", simply because God (Allah, Jahveh) has commanded it: Humans are not to eat pork, period! Sheep, not pig. Halal and kosher, not Western slaughter. And when it comes to attire: hijab for women, and no silk ties[32] for men! Well, personal preferences of this kind are one thing. Fair enough. But to claim that God, in a universe such as ours, with all of our huge problems and real challenges, should trouble himself with such matters, simply appears as odd. The universe in which we live is already from the outset an unstable and dangerous place to be, and we humans have created a risk-society, with overconsumption and overpopulation, which may lead to catastrophic conditions, where many will be in want of food and clothing. In the midst of all this, God should be particularly preoccupied with attires and cooking! For an enlightened person, this means that God lacks any sense of proportion, and thus he appears as foolish. In short, theologically speaking, this must be blasphemy of the worst kind.

Enlightened modern people would probably agree with what we have stated so far, but many will also emphasize that the Holy Scriptures and religious traditions still contain many valuable and morally relevant advices and commands.

---

30 We might see such taboos as an expression of an outdated socio-historical context. Therefore, the interpretations of the scriptures (and the traditions) must be critically historized. This point applies to a range of such commands and prohibitions, e.g. the view on blood in the Old Testament (as for Jehovah's Witnesses). If one claims that "the soul is in the blood", one begs several critical questions, from psychology to physiology.

31 Cf. our next point: the problem of blasphemy.

32 Mohammad Usman Rana informs in an interview (repeated in *Dagbladet magasinet*, 12.02.2010) that he cannot buy silk ties because Muslim men should not wear silk for religious reasons. So God is meticulous. (Again, this would pose a problem for the Chinese, who do not conceive silk and gender roles in this way).

To speak of God in light of the problem of evil **31**

And so it is. Both individually and collectively, religion and religious faith may demonstrably have a positive influence and important function.[33]

That said, there is, for historical reasons, *not much to be found* in these scriptures and traditions when it comes to addressing decidedly *modern challenges*, e.g. concerning the relationship between different social institutions (such as the State, the market, and the life world) and between different forms of rationality (e.g. discursive, interpretational, and instrumental reasons). In short, normative challenges that spring out of modern institutional and epistemic problematics require concepts and skills that simply are not present in these scriptures or traditions. They say nothing about nanotechnology or institutional differentiation. Instead, they have a few things to say about female slaves and slavery.

A lot of the contents of the scriptures are, in other words, *outdated* and *not very relevant*. The moral imperatives presented by these scriptures may therefore often be of limited relevance, or they might be outdated, such as the encouragement to *multiply and replenish the earth!* Yes, at the time, but today, the circumstances are completely different, when it comes to demography and ecological limitations. Or: *Whom the Lord loveth, he chastiseth!* But today, we know better, through enlightenment and through a "modernization of consciousness". Or: *Go and sell all you have and give the money to the poor!* All right, fine, if the point is to share equally and on the condition that we are all in the same situation and some have a lot and some have little,[34] but it is not so simple in today's society where we also have to consider a working economic life and other institutional preconditions.

In other words, it is necessary to maintain a tentative and critical attitude towards many of the prohibitions and commands that are mentioned in the Holy Scriptures. Some of the writings are outdated, and a lot of that which is important for our current societies is absent – it is simply not there. Therefore, all of it needs to be interpreted and updated.

This is, of course, old news for anyone who has paid attention. But in the current situation, with a multi-faceted revitalization of religion, many of those who are anchored in the three monotheistic religions are *not* aware of this. In this regard, we are not merely faced with the problem of theodicy based on the problem of evil, but also with a challenge for the monotheistic conception of God which we may refer to as "the problem of the ridiculous": As shown earlier, when we take everything in the scriptures and in the traditions seriously in an uncritical way, then God (Allah, Jahveh) may appear to be foolish.

---

33 This is a fundamental point for Jürgen Habermans, e.g. in *Zwischen Naturalismus und Religion*, Suhrkamp, Frankfurt a.M. 2005, English translation *Between Naturalism and Religion*, Wiley, 2014. For more on Habermas' perspective, see Part IV in this publication.
34 And not the least if one is under the conviction that we are living in the Last Days (as many were in the early days of Christianity).

32 Science and religion

Hence, it becomes difficult to take seriously the request that we respect (and not only understand on a socio-historical basis) the various odd (and often contradicting) rules of life that are provided in the name of God, concerning everything from pork and halal or kosher to hijab and silk ties.

And to the extent that there are normative tensions within or between the different monotheistic religions (and orientations) – or with other "comprehensive doctrines",[35] religious or secular[36] – there is an urgent need for universal norms that may regulate the interaction between different perceptions and beliefs.[37]

In other words, when we consider the problem of evil as it appears in the ideal-typical versions of the three monotheistic religions; and with a focus both on the core problems of God as almighty, omniscient, and benevolent; and on the different commands and prohibitions that define reprehensible or sinful behaviour, it is necessary[38] to take a step back and view the different perceptions in relation to each other and in relation to what we today think we know, based in different kinds of scientific and scholarly insight and historical learning processes.

Hence, I assume, it is not attractive, neither religiously nor theologically speaking, to be left with perceptions of God as tyrannical or foolish. The concept of God that we are then left with, and which stands up in a modern science-based society, is a more remote conception of God, epistemically and normatively – both with regard to what we can know and what we can say about God, and with regard to what God's word has to say to us, with relevance for our various challenges in modern precarious risk-societies.

This last point should not be interpreted as a restrictive and dismissive stance when it comes to the role of religion in providing meaning and direction in modern societies. Here Habermas has an important cultural-sociological point: It makes sense to view religion as a spiritual and moral force also in modern societies – and, I would add: especially in awe of vulnerable life, biologically as well as spiritually.

What implications does this have for the perception of the Holy?

With this, I have already hinted at my position when it comes to the relationship between faith and morality. They are connected, but not in the way that

---

35 Cf. John Rawls.
36 Whatever might be the interpretation of these terms.
37 Cf. "Religion and Modernity, 'modernization of consciousness' and the need for a criticism of religion'", in Gunnar Skirbekk, *Religion, Modernity, and Rationality*, SVT Press, Bergen 2006, pp. 9–29.
38 Necessary in the light of the plurality, and based in the contradictions between different perceptions within these monotheistic traditions, and furthermore in relation to the array of other religions and spiritual orientations.

many people seem to perceive it: that we through a literal reading of Holy Scriptures may gain finite answers to how we should organize ourselves in modern risk-societies. In this sense, 'faith alone' is not enough, not when it comes to morality and justice in our world. Discursive rationality[39] is a necessity, among other things – for us fallible creatures, who know only in part.

And as for the Holy? The Holy is traditionally deeply connected to *the eternal*. But are there not good reasons, not the least from the perspective of Christian tradition, to view the Holy in the *vulnerable and perishable* – that which is in need of compassion and protection, and which therefore calls for moral acts and attitudes?

Plato's eternal Ideal Forms need no morality; they are the same and will remain so throughout eternity. But for vulnerable lives it is different. That applies to the individual soul and body as well as to the spiritual and social communities. Here, morality is needed with a range of enlightened measures.

And who knows, perhaps we are not the only ones who are vulnerable? Might God also be vulnerable? Is this what is signalled by the life and suffering of Jesus?

Allahu Akbar, God is great – but *almighty and invulnerable*? Indeed, it does not appear so, seen from a chaotic risk-society in urgent crisis, quite a way from the harmonious universe that Leibniz envisioned in the early eighteenth century. And what is more, *eternal and unchangeable*? In principle, perhaps, but not as a person in the way we see persons: Someone who communicates with others, changes, and learns by doing. And *rigidly judgemental*, for all eternity? But everything in moderation, in the light of the problem of evil!

The problem of evil does not concern the question of God's existence. But the problem of evil, as is the case with "the problem of the ridiculous", is decisive for how we understand and speak of God. Those who neglect to acknowledge this easily come off as blasphemous, regardless of whether they themselves share this perception. They are unintentionally blasphemous. Such takes are understandable from a socio-historical and psychological perspective. But it does not call for extraordinary respect. Quite the contrary; based on active legislation on blasphemy, one might even claim that this could constitute a basis for legal prosecution.

---

39 Cf. e.g. reflections on the Holy Spirit in Gunnar Skirbekk, *Den filosofiske uroa*, Universitetsforlaget, Oslo 2005, pp. 174–183.

PART II

Religion and the constitutional state

3
FREEDOM OF EXPRESSION AND CARTOONS

With the vivid recollection of the controversy of the Muhammed cartoons, how can we justify the legal principle of freedom of expression, in a globalized world society?[1]

Three insufficient strategies of justification: (a) When providing a justification for freedom of expression, some will refer to *utility*: It is useful to have a legal principle of freedom of expression! True enough in many situations. But useful for whom? And what about the situations in which this principle would not, as it were, be 'useful'? (b) Some will claim that the *individual* is in principle free to express themselves; what is in need of justification, is the legal *delimitation* of this *individual liberty*. But in a globalized society, some perceive this liberty as a "Western value", not as a universally valid principle. (c) Others will maintain that we simply have to *decide* to be informed by the principle of freedom of expression. But this is *decisionism*, and it is poorly suited for providing a justification – for why could we not just decide to be informed by completely different principles?

---

1 This is a slightly revised version of a text that was presented at a meeting in the Norwegian Academy for the Sciences and the Arts on 9 November 2006. Published under the title «Ytringsfridom i ei globalisert verd» [Freedom of Expression in a Globalised World], in the yearbook of the Academy, in 2006, pp. 266–282, with illustrations p. 267. Cf. also Gunnar Skirbekk, «'Die Gedanken sind frei …'. Eine voraussetzungsanalytische Begründung des rechtlichen Schutzes der Meinungsfreiheit», *Philosophie der Moderne*, Velbrück Wissenschaft, Weilerswist 2017, pp. 69–85.

DOI: 10.4324/9781003441618-5

38 Religion and the constitutional state

Background

A justification of freedom of expression as a universally valid legal principle in a globalized and pluralistic society has to be *trans-contextual*. Referring to a specific tradition, a specific context, such as Norwegian or European legal practice, simply will not do. The cartoon controversy demonstrated this point: in a globalized world, with a wide range of traditions and "comprehensive doctrines",[2] we are faced with the question as to whether freedom of expression is merely a "Western value" or whether a trans-contextual justification of the freedom of expression, as a universally binding legal principle, is possible.[3]

In order to follow this discussion on the cartoon controversy, it might be convenient to know what it is that we are talking about. Anyone who is interested in taking a look at the drawings of Muhammed, published in the Danish newspaper Jyllands-Posten, may find them on Wikipedia under *Jyllands-Posten Muhammad cartoons controversy*.

Objections and arguments

The objections from Muslim communities against the cartoons and their publication may briefly be summarized as follows:

The cartoons are offensive towards Muslims. Already from the outset, they violate the prohibition of visually depicting the Prophet in Sunni Islam. Moreover, the Prophet is depicted in a negative way: This is insulting the Prophet. And as Muslims identify with the Prophet, it insults all Muslims. These are the religiously motivated reactions.

The publishing of the cartoons was a provocation to the Muslim population because many live in difficult conditions and because they have long perceived themselves as harassed by the West. This is the socio-politically motivated reaction.

The arguments for and against the publishing of the cartoons can be organized as three basic positions:

Freedom of expression is (merely) a "Western value"! This implies that freedom of expression is rejected as a universal principle. Such objections came from certain Asian countries and from representatives from Muslim communities.

---

2 "Comprehensive doctrines", cf. John Rawls, *Political Liberalism*, Columbia University Press, New York, 1993.

3 In the Freedom of Expression Commission, of which I was a member in 1993–1996, the matter at hand was primarily a revision of the Norwegian Constitution, Article 100. In this text, the issue is another one, more open and context-independent, both when it comes to the Norwegian legal tradition and the European Human Rights Convention.

Freedom of expression is "one value amongst many"! Therefore, the issue of freedom of expression must be weighed against other values, such as conviviality and the absence of bad feelings. This argument was broadly employed, also by Western representatives.

Freedom of speech applies "absolutely and without restrictions of any kind"! This argument was at times posed with the added assertion that all statements in principle deserve the same protection, whether they are non-verbal cartoons or thoroughly articulated expressions of opinion. This unrestricted pro-argument was *inter alia* put forth by certain high-profile media personalities.[4]

My counterarguments to these three positions are the following: (i) Freedom of expression is not merely a Western value. (ii) Nor is freedom of expression merely one value among many. (iii) Although it is possible to justify freedom of expression as a universally valid principle, some restrictions must be in place; moreover, it is not the case that all statements deserve the same protection.

Based on the question of how freedom of expression may be justified as a universally valid principle, I will in the following substantiate these three claims.

But first, I will briefly outline the difficulties connected to the justification of universally valid basic norms:

Such a justification cannot be *empirical*. In short, we cannot transition from *is* to *ought*.[5]

Such a justification cannot be *contextual*. We seek a trans-traditional, trans-contextual principle – contextual justifications will not do.

Nor will a traditional *metaphysical* or theological justification fulfil our purpose, for there is a range of different metaphysical and theological basic perceptions which are themselves in need of justification, and then we are back where we started – this point may constitute a foundation for philosophical scepticism.

Some might hold that the answer is to be found in *decisionism*. When it comes down to the essentials, normative justification is a matter of what we

---

4 Cf., e.g., Per Edgar Kokkvold, secretary-general of the Norwegian Press Association. Kokkvold, who received death threats, emphasized that caricatures deserve particular protection based in a principle of freedom of expression (as he stated in an interview, *inter alia* because caricatures provide a perspective which is "more true than reality").

5 We cannot pursue this problem in detail here, e.g. considering "institutional facts" (which carry normativity, such as "corner" in football), nor with regard to actual conditions (e.g. of an ecological nature), which, based in empirical arguments, can be said to be normatively binding if we want to avoid chaos and catastrophe. See the following chapters on "constitutive preconditions".

40 Religion and the constitutional state

decide! But if so, there are no limits to what we might decide, so neither will this approach do as a justification for freedom of speech as a universal principle.

Not empirical, neither contextual, nor metaphysical, nor decisionism. What then? With this reminder as our backdrop, we will take a closer look at *two central strategies of justification* for freedom of expression as a universally valid principle:

Justification of freedom of expression: a (self-evident) "innate and inalienable right" for all individuals

Cf., e.g., the statement about human rights in the U.S. declaration of July 4, 1776 (*A declaration by the representatives of the United States of America, in general congress assembled*):

> *We hold these truths to be self-evident; that all men are created equal; that they are endowed by their creator with (inherent and) inalienable rights; that among these are life, liberty, and the pursuit of happiness.*

We recognize these perceptions from political theory from Hobbes to Locke: there are certain fundamental rights, and these rights belong to the individual. All individuals are equal insofar as these rights apply to all of them. These rights provide protection against unlawful interference from the State. At the same time, this requires a political and legal system that may balance these rights between individuals.

In other words: In principle, an individual is free and autonomous. They have the right to express themselves. In principle, an individual holds freedom of expression for any kind of utterances.

But in practice, certain topics and certain kinds of utterances will stand out as more important than others when it comes to the right to freedom of expression. Thoroughly articulated public utterances concerning political, scientific, or religious issues will normally be considered to be of particular importance.

This strategy of justification immediately faces us with two potential problems: on the one hand, the appeal to self-evident truths, and on the other, the notion of the individual as free and independent, as autonomous.

The first problem is well-known from the criticism of rationalistic metaphysics[6]: Due to the range of perceptions with regard to what is to be taken as self-evidently true, we get a sceptical challenge based on this pluralism of metaphysical basic perceptions. This objection weighs heavily when we are aiming for a universally valid justification for the principle of freedom of expression.

The second problem concerns the relationship between the individual and society, between individualization and socialization (in the social-psychological sense). This too is a well-known problem in, e.g., political philosophy,

---

6 Rationalistic metaphysics, from Plato to Leibniz.

visible, e.g., in the tension between Hobbes and Locke on the one hand, and Burke or Hegel on the other. For the sake of brevity, we may here speak of a contrast between regarding individual *autonomy* as a (*postulated*) *fact* (in all humans or all persons) on the one hand, and regarding individual autonomy as an (*ongoing*) *project*, where we would speak in terms of more-or-less (not in terms of either-or).

A strong conviction about individual autonomy was in many ways a basic element in the 'modern project', as an ideal from the Enlightenment Age and its faith in progress, freedom, and reason, based on the idea of autonomous people, in the shape of free and reasonable, open and enlightened persons. But, as we know, these ideas were soon subjected to extensive criticism from several directions. The criticism was based on different kinds of empirical research, from biology to psychology to sociology to history but also on philosophical 'deconstruction' of the concepts of rationality and autonomy.[7]

In this sense, the emergence of the different scientific and scholarly disciplines can be said to undermine or at least have a crucial impact on the notion of humans as autonomous agents: It is problematic to speak of individual autonomy as an empirical fact, just as it is problematic to ascribe the same autonomy to all individuals.

Here it becomes necessary to distinguish between the state of belonging to *homo sapiens* as a species and the state of being a responsible and autonomous person, just as it is necessary to distinguish between empirical facts and ideal normative preconditions. In short, we must take seriously the criticism against the project of modernization. By extension, we are also faced with the objection that the project of modernization is basically a "Western" endeavour, which is not universally valid. And so, the problem complex itself becomes politically explosive, in today's globalized society.

What we have outlined so far, is a quite common strategy of justification for freedom of expression. It represents a typical approach to the question of how freedom of expression is to be understood, and of how we may justify the freedom of expression as a universally valid, trans-contextual norm: The individual holds unalienable rights, including freedom of expression! But here we are (as mentioned) faced with different kinds of objections: philosophical, empirical, and geo-political.

Justification of freedom of expression: based on the pursuit of truth, autonomy, and (deliberative) democracy

Cf., e.g., the Norwegian Constitution's "justification of the freedom of expression"[8] as grounded in "the seeking of truth, the promotion of democracy and

---

7 Central names include Darwin, Nietzsche, and Freud. But in particular, we are talking about a 'soberization' (of the notion of the autonomous person) through research within disciplines that concern themselves with causal explanation and contextualization.
8 NOU 27/1999, p. 27.

42 Religion and the constitutional state

the individual's freedom to form opinions", where these three justifications (truth-seeking, autonomy, and democracy) are seen as interrelated. This is basically a common approach to a justification of the freedom of expression.

Historically, this strategy of justification is situated in the Enlightenment Age: Enlightenment (*Aufklärung*) means that fallible and reasonable persons, who are sufficiently autonomous, test different perceptions of public issues through sensible discussion (which also includes mutual role-taking). The point is this: In order to claim that one is (reasonably) right, one must be familiar with the counterarguments. Those who seek the better argument must be open towards sensible counterarguments. This is why freedom of expression is necessary: Freedom of expression is an indispensable *precondition* for discursive rationality – it is not merely a Western value and not simply a value among other values. Cf. John Stuart Mill in *On Liberty* (1859)[9]:

> There is the greatest difference between presuming an opinion to be true, because, with every opportunity for contesting it, it has not been refuted, and assuming its truth for the purpose of not permitting its refutation. Complete liberty of contradicting and disproving our opinion, is the very condition which justifies us in assuming its truth for purposes of action; and on no other terms can a being with human faculties have any rational assurance of being right.

For us humans, as fallible creatures, the freedom of expression is a necessary precondition for the ability to distinguish between unreasonable and reasonable convictions. This is the point. We might well talk about freedom of expression as a 'value', and as a 'utility', but that misses the crucial aspect: For creatures who depend upon open discussion that brings to light arguments and counterarguments, for such creatures, freedom of expression is an indispensable precondition for the seeking of truth and for the individual's freedom to form opinions.

This applies to all serious discussions where we seek the better arguments, whether in scientific and scholarly discussions, such as in a doctoral defence, or in a public deliberation about matters concerning the general population.

With regard to the discussion of public matters, it is crucial that all parties and their different perspectives are heard in the public sphere, that counterarguments are taken seriously, and that the public discourse does not exclude certain (kinds of) people who are affected by the issue at hand and who have views on the matter.

In this sense, we can say that democracy as an ideal is founded upon the precondition of a deliberative forming of opinions among persons who are

---

9 Chapter II, "Of Liberty of Thought and Discussion".

Freedom of expression and cartoons **43**

fallible and vulnerable, but who, notwithstanding, are autonomous enough to be able to take responsibility for their own lives and to be included in public discourse on matters that concern them.

The deliberative forming of opinions serves to eliminate unreasonable and unattainable perceptions and may at the same time serve as a mutual and formative learning-process among the participants. In turn, this forming of opinion may inform a vote on different issues and initiatives that have been thus purged, among persons who are themselves shaped by such cultivating processes of socialization. In short, democracy applies to persons who are at the same time fallible, autonomous, and vulnerable. (Democracy is not for animals or incorporeal angels.)

In this way, we can talk about the justification of freedom of expression in the seeking of truth, the promotion of democracy and the individual's freedom to form opinions, and the interconnectedness of these justifications. Freedom of expression appears as an indispensable precondition for truth-seeking discourse aiming at valid perceptions, and therefore also for deliberative democracy and for the freedom to form opinions and cultivation of autonomous persons.

Freedom of expression as constitutive precondition for discursive seeking of truth

When it comes down to the essentials, this justification for freedom of expression as a universally valid principle is *not* empirical, *not* deductive, *not* rationalistically 'top-down'. When it comes down to the essentials, the argumentation is reflective and self-critical in the sense that it would be a performative contradiction to argue seriously and at the same time reject the principle of freedom of expression. This justification for freedom of expression is 'bottom-up' because it reveals inherent preconditions for our discursive speech acts in a reflecting way: Freedom of expression appears as an indispensable procedural norm for serious discussion.

We have now provided a justification for freedom of expression as a universal norm, as a universally valid principle, and not merely as a "Western value", not merely as a contextually contingent principle. But is this justification not still contextually contingent? Well, it is included in a contextual precondition in the sense that freedom of expression is an indispensable precondition for serious discussion. But the crucial point is this: Serious discussion is not an arbitrary activity or a context that we are at liberty to disregard. Anyone who wishes to argue against what we have stated here must engage in a serious discussion, and thus presuppose the constitutive conditions for such a discussion, including the principle of freedom of expression.

The discussion is precisely the context in which we found ourselves when we engage in discussion. That is the crucial point. And we should add that the activity of discussing is included in all forms of scientific practice; we are

44 Religion and the constitutional state

here speaking of extensive and central institutions in modern societies, which transition to public discourse and educational institutions.

Therefore, it makes no sense to talk about the principle of freedom of expression as a contextual norm as if we were at liberty to accept or reject this principle. Quite the contrary, we may say that freedom of expression is a universally valid principle for anyone who wishes to express themselves in serious discourse about what is right and true.

Autonomy as a project

It is worth noting that this strategy of justification for freedom of expression as a universally valid principle is based on a notion of humans as fallible creatures who only know in part, and that we, precisely for this reason, depend on each other in discursive truth-seeking and the freedom to form opinions. In this sense, we are here operating with a robust perspective of human life that does not take human autonomy as a given fact (as is the case in the first strategy of justification in this chapter), but where the issue of autonomy is seen as an ongoing project which requires individual effort as well as learning processes in interplay with others.

The discursive formation of opinion as a core area

Based on this strategy of justification, serious discussions, public discourse, and the individual's freedom to form opinions constitute what we may see as the core utterances covered by the freedom of expression. At the same time, we should acknowledge that this justification is an *addition* to other arguments that can be posed in support of the freedom of expression. It does not exclude that freedom of expression might be "useful" in certain situations and that freedom of expression in various contexts might be referred to as a "value".[10] In this sense, our justification of freedom of expression does not subtract anything but adds something (resulting in a strong protection of freedom of expression).

But this protection applies particularly to a *core area*, which is granted the strongest protection, with a gradual protection as one moves away from this core area and towards other kinds of utterances. Utterances that are far from serious discourse – such as commercial utterances, porn, or violent movies – will have a weaker protection.

This as opposed to the first strategy of justification in this chapter, where freedom of expression is taken as an innate right applying to all individuals. But this justification too would in practice typically involve a gradual protection where certain utterances would be considered more important than others when it comes to the freedom of expression.

---

10 Cf. the introductory remarks about three common strategies of justification and their relative relevance.

Therefore, it may *in practice* still be significant convergence between the two strategies of justification: The individual-based strategy will in practice distinguish between central and peripheral utterances, and the discourse-based strategy will expand the perspective by including utterances that are far from discursive utterances.

The need for free utterances beyond discursive utterances

There are two reasons why it makes sense to expand the perspective in this way. First, this strategy (as mentioned) opens for the different value-based assessments of freedom of expression; such assessments are not eliminated. Second, such discursive utterances do not originate nor prevail in a vacuum: A sensible discussion depends on several factors – cultural, emotional, and developmental. In order to be able to engage in discussion, one, e.g., needs a firm and flexible identity – flexible enough to be able to recognize the better arguments and firm enough to be able to withstand biased and unreasonable expectations and pressure. Hence, what is needed is a "modernization of consciousness."[11] And this may e.g. mean that it is good or useful to have freedom of artistic expressions, with bold statements that are not necessarily thoroughly articulated, or to have emotional outbursts. The extent to which this would be useful is a scientific (empirical) issue. The point is that what is needed is an expansion of the protection of the freedom of expression so that it encompasses much more than serious discursive utterances, precisely in order to ensure that such discursive utterances originate and prevail.

Closing remarks

With this, we close the discussion of the two strategies of justification for the freedom of expression as a universally valid principle across cultures and traditions. As is clear from these discussions, I favour the latter of the two strategies.

But in addition to the problem of justification comes the question of different *kinds* of utterances and of the different *fora* within which they take place – such circumstances are also of importance for assessing, e.g., the Muhammed cartoons.

Different kinds of utterances and different kinds of protection

Based on the latter strategy of justification, it is first and foremost discursive utterances that receive full protection from the principle of freedom of

---

11 Again, this expression is borrowed from Jürgen Habermas, *Zwischen Naturalismus und Religion*, Suhrkamp, Frankfurt a.M. 2005, e.g., p. 146. /English translation 2008. *Between Naturalism and Religion: Philosophical essays*. Polity, Cambridge, e.g., p. 136.

46 Religion and the constitutional state

expression. Beyond this, it would be an empirical endeavour to determine what other kinds of utterances should be included – utterances that may contribute to an insightful and tolerant culture, which may be seen as having value in itself or as useful for an open public conversation. Hence, for instance, artistic utterances of different kinds might deserve protection from the principle of freedom of expression. But then again, some kinds of artistic expressions might in practice turn out to have a *negative effect* on the preconditions for an open public conversation. Determining whether the effect is negative or positive would be an empirical endeavour. Therefore, the protection of artistic expressions has a different and more uncertain status than the protection of what we refer to as the core area of discursive utterances.

Likewise, an assessment of the protection of commercial utterances should be informed by a similar line of reasoning. In this regard, it is, e.g., important to have a view to the paradigmatic distinction between *communicative* (including discursive) utterances and *instrumental* utterances, while in practice there are all kinds of transitions. This is important since extreme versions of instrumental utterances, such as systematic *indoctrination* and *manipulation*, may undermine personal autonomy and thus come into conflict with one of the preconditions for freedom of expression. Rather than deserving protection based on the principle of freedom of expression, it might be the case that, e.g., *religious and ideological indoctrination* (as well as political advertisements and propaganda) in practice constitute utterances that undermine an important precondition for freedom of expression, such as a certain degree of personal autonomy, and that such utterances should be rejected, in the name of freedom of expression. Demonstrably brutalizing violent movies will be included in the same category.

These are the extreme cases of instrumental utterances. *Commercial utterances*, of different kinds, will also include instrumental utterances, but normally of a moderate kind. Here the issue is primarily a question of what role the market institution, and its strategic utterances, should play in a modern institutionally differentiated society.

Different fora and different kinds of protection

When assessing the degree of protection based in the principle of freedom of expression, it is furthermore important to consider the different fora and settings in which the utterances appear. Is it in writing – in books and newspapers, or on billboards and in public places? Or are they visual, such as in movies, photography, or different kinds of visual arts? Or do they come in the shape of sounds, such as in normal speech or other sound effects? Or in combinations of all this?

We recall: Books must be bought or borrowed and then read. The same is true for newspapers, but this often involves a subscription, so that a reader might to a greater extent be exposed to unwanted utterances. And with televised advertisements, people are to an even greater extent exposed to utterances that they would not normally seek out.

Utterances will behave differently in different fora and settings depending on whether we have sought them out actively and voluntarily or whether we have been passively and involuntarily exposed to them. In the hypothetical case in which a researcher were to think that the Prophet was a paedophile, it would be an immense difference between publishing this opinion in a scientific journal or exposing it through audio-visual utterances on prime-time television.[12]

Limits to the freedom of expression

"There are limits to the freedom of expression!" Yes, three types:

1 There are limits to the freedom of expression when utterances *undermine* that which constitutes *the justification for freedom of expression*. Expressing oneself in a way that undermines the personal autonomy of others represents a paradigmatic case of utterances that should be suspended, precisely with reference to the principle of freedom of expression. We may here refer to the previously mentioned threefold justification in the Norwegian Constitution pertaining to the pursuit of truth, democracy, and the individual freedom to form opinions.

Moreover, regardless of the strategy for justification, we are here, broadly speaking, dealing with two kinds of delimitations to the freedom of expression: cases of defamation and slander, and cases of utterances that may lead to a fatal destabilization of society, such as war and terror.

2 When it comes to defamation and slander, it is worth noting that: If defamation takes the shape of an utterance that approaches an *undermining of the personal autonomy of others*, we are immediately faced with a delimitation of the protection based on the principle of freedom of expression.

Then again, we must acknowledge that personal autonomy requires us to take responsibility for what we do and say, and to remain open to criticism of actions and attitudes that may be reprehensible in one way or another. For instance, if one, out of excessive respect for another, refrains from offering fair and reasonable criticism, one does, in effect, *not* acknowledge the other as an autonomous person – quite the contrary, one reduces the other *qua* autonomous and responsible person.

In this context, we often hear the argument that we should not express ourselves in a way that offends the religious feelings of others, particularly when it comes to persons representing other traditions and faiths than our own. This makes sense to some extent. But these kinds of emotions are not

---

12 Or posting it on social media.

48 Religion and the constitutional state

natural phenomena, which are just there on their own accord. Such emotions are connected to perceptions and convictions which may in many cases be subjected to debate and which may thus appear as more-or-less reasonable.[13] The argument that we should not express ourselves in a way that offends or provokes the religious feelings of others is thus ambiguous.

Moreover, there are many convictions in modern pluralistic societies that may trigger emotions in those who profess to these convictions. This does not only apply to the three monotheistic religions with all their branches but includes a number of other religions, in addition to atheists and agnostics who have their own convictions and accompanying emotions. And at times, political convictions may have an equal status. With this, it becomes difficult to express oneself at all, as one would always be in danger of offending one group or other and their emotionally charged convictions.

In some situations, moreover, many would consider it necessary to criticize convictions and offend the accompanying emotions – as was the case in full measure towards the national socialists after World War II.

All in all, this means that there are good grounds to be cautious when delimiting the freedom of expression based on the objection that the utterances may result in defamation and hurt feelings.

3 We are now left with the objections based on the real danger of *fatal destabilization* of society, possibly *war* and *terror*. This is, of course, a strong argument from the point of view of practical politics, notably when there is reason to claim that the danger is real. In order to assess whether this is the case, both good insight and good political judgement are needed. Taken to the extremes, this can be related to the dilemma in Munich in 1938: When should we go along, with hopes of "peace for our time," and when should we put our foot down and stand our ground? Such considerations are notoriously difficult.

What then, about the Muhammed cartoons? This was the point of departure for our reflections on the justification of the freedom of expression as a universal principle, valid across traditions and religious orientations.

What about the Muhammed cartoons?

We recall how the cartons looked and where they were published. Based on the reflections earlier in this chapter, it might be worthwhile to make a few

---

13 Hence, all of the three monotheistic religions (Judaism, Christianity, and Islam) contain central validity claims (e.g. regarding God as creator and norm-provider) which may and should be subjected to discussion and which have indeed been discussed for hundreds of years. Cf., e.g., Gunnar Skirbekk, "Religion and Modernity. 'Modernization of consciousness' and the need for a criticism of religion", in *Religion, Modernity, and Rationality*, SVT Press, Bergen 2006 (pp. 9–31).

brief observations about the controversy surrounding these cartoons. We do this based on the premise that freedom of expression is a universal norm, with discursive utterances as its core area and with gradual expansion to other kinds of utterances. The following observations are not taken to be comprehensive, nor professional in the legal sense of the word.

The prohibition against visual depiction. The prohibition against visual representation of the Prophet (including cases where He is depicted in a positive way), applies to large parts of the Muslim population, but not to all Muslims. In a pluralistic global society, we furthermore find a wide range of religious convictions, from Buddhism and animism to charismatic movements and satanism. Moreover, there is no reason why we should limit ourselves to religious convictions (as the term is notoriously equivocal), in which case we have to include all other deeply felt convictions. If everyone were to pay heed to all prohibitions that all of these different and to some extent contradictory orientations operate with, we would find ourselves in an impossible predicament. In short, in a globalized and pluralistic world, it is virtually impossible to avoid violating some prohibition or other that exists in some conviction or other. We should then add that the principle of freedom of expression opens for the freedom of religion, but also for the critique of religion, for criticizing religious and ideological convictions and acts. In this perspective, the freedom of religion does not mean freedom from criticism, but freedom to criticize.

Negative depictions. The issue in question, the Muhammed cartoons, consists of 12 cartoons. Not all of them depict the Prophet. Some of them are good-natured. Perhaps only one of the drawings depicts the Prophet in a negative way (the one where He carries a bomb in his turban). The cartoons were published in a Danish newspaper. In order to be exposed to the drawings, one would have to perform a voluntary activity. The cartoons were not forced upon a passive audience, as would be the case with public billboards or a sudden television appearance.

Provoking large groups who already feel offended. In a globalized world, utterances that were initially presented in a local context may soon become widely known. Such was also the case in this instance. But what was particular to this situation was that the distribution was carried out in specific ways, by specific actors, who on top of everything chose to add a picture of a French pig snout, which was bound to stir up hostile feelings. In this sense, the controversy was staged. Then again, one might argue that the reactions were a result of a collective frustration that had built up over time due to circumstances such as poor living conditions and a feeling of being repeatedly humiliated by the West. But in that case, the appropriate response from the West would be to change

50 Religion and the constitutional state

the policy towards the afflicted areas, e.g. in the conflict between Israel and Palestine. Compromising freedom of expression would simultaneously be problematic on the level of principles and insufficient on the level of politics. (One would address the symptom rather than the decisive underlying cause.) Finally, one might ask whether the miserable conditions in the many Muslim states may be rooted in local circumstances and not only in Western policy and Western intrusion.[14] Furthermore, we must also ask whether religion, in its local variations, may be co-responsible for the underlying problems in these countries. All in all, it is therefore not very likely that obstructing the freedom of expression and shutting down critiques of religion would be the most appropriate response to the argument that large population groups reacted when they heard of the Muhammed cartoons because they were frustrated with the circumstances that prevail where they live.

Respecting the emotions of others. But should we not respect the emotions of others? Yes and no. As previously mentioned, we must distinguish between reasonable and unreasonable emotions. And as mentioned earlier, all kinds of emotions exist in pluralistic societies. Some of which are contradictory. It is therefore virtually impossible to pay heed to all of them. Precisely for this reason, it is necessary to distinguish between religion and the legal system.[15] And precisely for this reason, we need critique of religion (in the Kantian sense), as a part of the process of the "modernization of consciousness". And for that reason, it is important to be able to refer to a justification of the freedom of expression that is universally valid, across traditions and cultures.

Real danger of a destabilized society, possibly of war and terrorist attacks. This is the toughest question. There are utterances that in certain situations may trigger fatal events. Whether this is the case, must be carefully assessed in each individual situation. When it comes down to the essentials, it is a task for the political leadership, in correspondence with the citizens in an open public discourse and in collaboration with a vast array of expertise, along with a competent intelligence service. But in such cases as well, we must expect the prime minister and the minister of foreign affairs to stand tall in the defence of freedom of expression as an indispensable precondition for truth-seeking, democracy, and the individual's freedom to form opinions.

*

14 Cf. Ahmet T. Kuru on this issue in Part IV in this chapter.
15 In a rule of law, all citizens are subject to the same legal system, regardless of their religious affiliation.

Appendix

The Norwegian Constitution Article 100

There shall be freedom of expression.

No one may be held liable in law for having imparted or received information, ideas, or messages unless this can be justified in relation to the grounds for freedom of expression, which are the seeking of truth, the promotion of democracy, and the individual's freedom to form opinions. Such legal liability shall be prescribed by law.

Everyone shall be free to speak their mind frankly on the administration of the State and on any other subject whatsoever. Clearly defined limitations to this right may only be imposed when particularly weighty considerations so justify in relation to the grounds for freedom of expression.

Prior censorship and other preventive measures may not be applied unless so required in order to protect children and young persons from the harmful influence of moving pictures. Censorship of letters may only be imposed in institutions.

Everyone has a right of access to documents of the State and municipalities and a right to follow the proceedings of the courts and democratically elected bodies. Limitations to this right may be prescribed by law to protect the privacy of the individual or for other weighty reasons.

The authorities of the State shall create conditions that facilitate open and enlightened public discourse.

4

OFFENCE, THE LIMIT OF FREEDOM OF EXPRESSION?[1]

The legal delineation for the freedom of expression includes two kinds of utterances: utterances that are likely to lead to violent and chaotic situations and utterances that to a great extent violate the right to privacy.

Therefore, when a person is seriously offended by a specific utterance, the freedom of expression may be restricted. But in modern liberal democracies, this only applies to *living people*, not to the dead, not to theories, not to traditions or cultures, not to confessions nor religions. It applies to living persons as a defence for their self-esteem, identity, and autonomy. Still, it is conceivable that harsh and persistent criticism of a specific group's *cultural background* would seriously offend this group and hurt them as autonomous persons.

In cases of offence, it is not merely a matter of what is stated, but of *the way in which* it is uttered. The manner is important. One and the same statement may be uttered either aggressively or with respect and empathy. The *place* is also important. And here, as is so often the case, it makes sense to distinguish between statements that we are *randomly and involuntarily* exposed to (such as advertisements and propaganda) and statements that we voluntarily and through our own efforts seek out (such as books and magazines). Moreover, technological innovation and social media have in recent years revolutionized the entire field. More people participate, with no editorial safeguard. Thus, public discourse has become more irreconcilable and cruder, and characterized by, e.g., offensive verbal attacks and insults.

---

1 A slightly revised version of a text published in *Bergens Tidende*, on 17 March 2020.

DOI: 10.4324/9781003441618-6

But here we are faced with a problem, as the claim to offence caused by certain utterances may function as a *power strategy*, as a trump card, which effectively kills the debate. Hence, the proposal of a United Nations resolution to condemn the defamation of religion – because the critique of religion is said to offend Islam, offend the Prophet, the Qur'an, and the feelings of Muslims.

What is more, the terminology is *not unequivocal*: Statements that are said to offend others, by hurting deep emotions and offending identity and autonomy, are the kind of statements that often contain *equivocal* expressions which are open to different interpretations. Likewise, there are different concepts of what it means to be insulted and what it means to be offended.

We will address two such concepts: (i) Offence through utterances that are experienced as provoking and that provoke *bad feelings*: anger, rage, discouragement, and a feeling of being hurt. (ii) Offence through utterances that *break down and destroy another individual's personal autonomy*, through brainwashing, indoctrination, manipulation, harassment.

Offence (i)

Feelings and emotions are crucial to this first concept. Cf. the Norwegian Prime Minister at the time, whose response to the violence in the Muslim world during the controversy of the Muhammed cartoons published in the Danish newspaper Jyllands-Posten in the fall of 2005: "It is important that we show respect for other people's feelings". [2]

But feelings are not an unequivocal phenomenon. There is, for instance, a difference between sensory impressions, feelings, and moods, where the two latter ones in different ways are influenced by social and cultural factors. In short, *sensory impressions* are 'given', physically, physiologically, or in other ways; *feelings* and *moods*, however, are contingent on cultures and traditions, or on religious faith and other fundamental convictions which are not shared by all. Moreover, feelings and moods may depend on our personal perception of a certain situation or our stance towards controversial religious and metaphysical issues. In other words, in some cases (but not in all cases), we have a responsibility for the feelings and moods we experience – either as a result of failing to avoid certain activities or situations or because we should have behaved as more mature and enlightened people with regard to our own attitudes and perceptions.

Frankly put: Those who feel offended and insulted by utterances made by other people, should not always be granted a veto. In other words: We should not always respect other people's feelings.

---

2 In the newspaper *VG-net*, on 6 February 2006.

54 Religion and the constitutional state

Offence (ii)

In this case, we are talking about degrading other people by breaking down their autonomy, either explicitly, through bullying and harassment, or more elusively through manipulation and indoctrination. The latter includes commercial advertisement and strategic political communication but also religious preaching which aims to shape others – particularly children and adolescents – in a certain way. Freedom of religion, yes, for teachers and preachers, but what about those who are shaped in this way? What about the children? They may be shaped, even brainwashed, in a way that impedes independent reflection and personal autonomy at a later stage, when they have grown into adults. This is an important point, but it is often neglected in the ongoing debate on freedom of expression and freedom of religion.

As a reminder: two statements from Ludvig Holberg:

> Children must be made into human beings before they become Christians; ... But we begin by the catechization of divine secrets, and as a result everyone defends with extreme obstinacy the sect in which he has been brought up and is not receptive to any arguments, at a later stage. ...[3]
>
> If one learns theology before one learns to become a human being, one will never become a human being.[4]

Of course, children are always raised in some socio-cultural context or other. The problem arises when these processes of socialization take the shape of indoctrination that undermines the personal autonomy of the person in question. True enough, this is not a widespread problem for religious people who are culturally modern, such as is typically the case in Western Europe, but elsewhere it is surely an issue. And this point, about manipulation and brainwashing, is not negligible. To break down the autonomy of another person through verbal manipulation and indoctrination is often, and rightly so, seen as a mortal sin. In many ways, this is far worse than making statements that lead to rage and anger.

In addition, we recall that offending a person's autonomy, to impede the freedom to form opinions, is a violation of the very justification for freedom of expression, normatively speaking, as it is defined in Article 100 of the Norwegian Constitution.

---

3 *Moralske Tanker*, F. J. Billeskov Jansen, Det Danske Sprog- og Litteraturselskab, København 1992, p. 35. English translation: *Moral reflections and epistles*, ed. P.M. Mitchell, 1991, pp. 13–14.
4 *Moralske tanker*, Libr. I, Epigr. 5, ed. G. Robe, 1859, pp. 43–44. English translation: *Moral reflections and epistles*, ed. P.M Mitchell, 1991, p. 15.

PART III

Religion and modern institutions

5

MULTICULTURALISM AND THE WELFARE STATE?[1]

Background

Is multiculturalism a challenge for the Nordic welfare state? The answer to this question depends on how we understand 'multiculturalism' and 'welfare state'. Hence, these terms need to be interpreted. Moreover, I will not in this chapter engage in empirical discussions on multiculturalism and welfare states, such as attitudes and trends in integration and work life.[2] As a philosopher of science, I will primarily engage with conceptual issues which are normally not addressed by empirical social research, but which nonetheless are of importance. (a) It concerns the limits to multiculturalism in cases where societal institutions and cultural identity are closely related; (b) it concerns the cultural diversity of science-based societies; (c) it concerns science-related problems that emerge in a religious defence of multiculturalism; (d) it concerns arguments in favour of a long-term perspective with an awareness of conflict when the relationship between multiculturalism and the welfare state is to be assessed.

But first, an informal reflection, after a trip to Beirut – with particular relevance for (a) and (d):

As it happened, I went to Lebanon on Easter, some years ago, in the company of Walid al-Kubaisi and his friends. The textbook on the history of philosophy was to be launched, a book which has travelled the Silk Road

---

1 A previous version of this text has been published in Norwegian in *Tidsskrift for velferdsforskning*, 2/2012; revised versions in *Religion og verdigrunnlaget for samfunnet*, publ. Hans Bringeland et al., 2014, and *Krise og medansvar*, 2016. This is a revised version of the latter publication.

2 But my discussion here will be relevant for legal discussions about multiculturalism in defence of collective rights for minorities (as opposed to individual rights, cf., e.g., William Kymlicka, *Multicultural citizenship*, Clarendon Press, Oxford 1995 *vs*. Brian Barry, *Culture and Equality*, Polity Press, Cambridge 2001).

DOI: 10.4324/9781003441618-8

58 Religion and modern institutions

from the East to the West, from Beijing to Beirut – in Chinese, Tajik, Uzbek, Azerbaijani, Russian, Turkish, and now Arabic. Beirut is said to have been a beautiful city. But civil war and conflict have taken its toll. We see it in refugee camps and quarters dominated by either Sunni Muslims, Shia Muslims, or Christians in various versions. We see it in houses, old and new, and we see it in the infrastructure: The metro system was broken, there was no tram, and buses were few and far between. But cars were everywhere. Therefore, traffic was slow, with a lot of noise and pollution. So I decided to walk from my hotel to the publishing house. But I got lost. Friendly people were eager to help, but I still did not find my way. Eventually, a Lebanese businessman invited me into his car. He was originally from Beirut and had emigrated to the United States with his family at the age of 7, where he had stayed for about 30 years, but now he was back in Beirut with his wife and four children. Traffic was slow, so we had time to talk about most things, from family and children to life in the United States and here in Lebanon. On the top of it all, he emphasized two points: It was good to be back in Lebanon, because here, one didn't pay taxes. And, "Don't trust anybody".

No taxes and no trust – what happens then during sickness or old age? The rich pay for private services; for the others, it is a disaster – but then again, so my local friends tell me: money comes from abroad. Iran supports Hezbollah, who in turn runs social initiatives in the Shia-dominated quarters, but not without expectations of reciprocation. Saudi Arabia supports the Sunnis, and the Christians might perhaps receive support from France and other Western countries.

A weak state, low degrees of trust, and credal division throughout the society. What then? Without a functioning tax system and with weak public institutions, clientism and clan loyalty become a way of life and a strategy for survival. Family honour and socio-religious loyalty become vital values; they constitute a cultural identity which is functionally reasonable in a society characterized by weak governmental and socio-political institutions. In short, we are here dealing with a kind of extreme multiculturalism and no welfare state.

The Nordic welfare state – a "model"?

It is quite common to refer to *the Nordic welfare state* as a "model".[3] Such a use of language makes sense in a range of academic disciplines: organization

---

3 In this chapter, I focus on the Nordic (Scandinavian) welfare state. At times, however, I refer exclusively to the Norwegian welfare state and its inherent preconditions. When addressing the Nordic (Scandinavian) welfare state, we normally refer to universal welfare benefits (in case of illness or other health issues, and old age and reduced capacity for work, with support for families with children and for the unemployed) and measures of social equity (through subsidies and tax policy), with variations over time and between countries. Cf., e.g., Nanna Kildal and Stein Kuhnle, eds., *Normative Foundations of the Welfare State: The Nordic experience*, Routledge, London 2007.

theory, law, and economics.[4] But if we define the Nordic welfare state as an organizational model, we are immediately confronted with a few challenging questions: How can it be that it is mainly in North-Western Europe, and particularly in the Nordic (Scandinavian) countries, that this kind of welfare state has emerged, and where does it appear to work best? If we are merely talking about a successful and detached model, then why haven't other states been successful in implementing these kinds of welfare measures? In order to answer these kinds of questions, we need other disciplinary perspectives than the aforementioned. It is then reasonable to turn to history, preferably with a focus on specific kinds of cultural and institutional modernization and socio-political learning processes.

In recent years, many scholars have based their work on such historical perspectives of modernization theory,[5] based *inter alia* in the hypothesis that the Scandinavian welfare state has its roots in a contentious interplay between national variants of Lutheran Protestantism and successful popular movements dating back to the early nineteenth century.[6] This question cannot be answered in a satisfactory manner through organizational concepts alone. What is needed is historical perspectives with a view to modernization theory.

In the Norwegian context, it is reasonable to look at the development of institutions and learning processes, over time, e.g., from the eighteenth century through the nineteenth century and into the twentieth century. Within such a perspective, it makes sense to focus on the emergence of legal institutions and a knowledge-based political administration, on the rule of law and a general willingness to follow the law, on Enlightenment ideals and popular education, on popular self-organization and socio-political learning processes.[7] Such concepts are relevant when we want to understand the contentious processes of modernization in political fora and in the public sphere, towards the introduction of parliamentary democracy and political parties in 1884, when the state officials abdicated peacefully, in the confidence that the nation would prevail under the rule of the parliamentary majority.

In short, in spite of class struggles and socio-cultural turbulence, by 1884 (after 70 years), both parties had acquired a basic trust towards each other

---

4 The Scandinavian welfare state is often referred to as a "model" in a *normative* sense, as an ideal that others try to live up to, or an ideal that they (in our view!) should try to live up to.

5 Cf. e.g. Øystein Sørensen and Bo Stråth, eds., *The Cultural Construction of Norden*, Scandinavian University Press, Oslo 1997, and Johann Arnason and Björn Wittrock, publ., *Nordic Paths to Modernity*, Berghahn Books, New York/Oxford 2012.

6 Many countries have a history of popular movements, cf., e.g., the labour movement and *die Jugendbewegung* in the German regions. But few have been *successful* in the sense that they have had a lasting effect on class relations and national culture, as they have in Scandinavia.

7 Cf. e.g. Gunnar Skirbekk, *Multiple Modernities. A Tale of Scandinavian Experiences*, The Chinese University Press, Hong Kong 2011, pp. 19–44.

60 Religion and modern institutions

and towards institutional procedures. Moreover, the material disparities were relatively moderate (compared to most other countries). In sum, this development paved the ground for a relatively egalitarian political culture, with a certain degree of mutual acknowledgement and a certain extent of general solidarity. The early twentieth century saw legislation reforms, promoted by Member of Parliament Johan Castberg, organizing and ensuring rights in work life and in family life, and despite crises and an intensified class struggle, the relationship between capital and labour (and between farmers and workers) was stabilized in the interwar period, which paved the ground for a crucial premise of the Nordic model: the relationship between employers, employees, and politicians. In short, the institutional and cultural preconditions for the establishment of the universal welfare state had been established well before the initiation of the universal welfare state as it occurred in the post-World War II years.[8]

If we want to address the welfare state from a perspective of organizational theory, we should thus add that the Nordic welfare state rests on *specific socio-cultural and political preconditions* – preconditions which have historical roots, which did not just appear on their own accord, and which may degenerate. Alternatively, we may choose a *more comprehensive notion* of the welfare state where, e.g., trust, solidarity, and the willingness to follow laws are integrated into the concept itself, along with ideals of personal autonomy, *inter alia* through self-organization,[9] education,[10] and popular enlightenment.[11]

---

8 On this note, we may refer to various socio-cultural preconditions for the Norwegian welfare state. I provide here a brief list of a range of interplaying factors: experience-based trust towards other people and towards political procedures and thereby trust in the rule of law and a willingness to follow the law, on the basis of a common public school system available to everyone (*folkeskole*) and popular enlightenment (*folkeopplysning*), a relatively transparent public sphere and socio-political learning-processes based in self-organisation in popular movements, from the early nineteenth century in a turbulent interplay with Lutheran state officials and in moderate economic disparities. As a result, a relatively egalitarian political culture emerged, in spite of class struggles and socio-cultural tensions, in short, national and general solidarity, with distinct counter- and multicultural dimensions (e.g. Norway operates with two forms of Norwegian written language), but based in a Danish-Norwegian version of Lutheran Protestantism. Within this expanded perspective, the normative basis of the welfare state may be referred to as a twofold ideal of personal autonomy and trust-based solidarity. Cf Skirbekk, *Multiple Modernities*, 2011.
9 Which is different from the neoliberal notion of freedom of choice, cf., e.g., Skirbekk 2011, pp. 166–167.
10 Cf. Nanna Kildal and Stein Kuhnle, publ., in *Normative Foundations of the Welfare State*, Routledge, London 2005, p. 17, "If we consider education as part of the welfare state, the Nordic countries stand out as relatively early proponents of a universal education. An early step towards democratization and universalization of education was the demand for general literacy for all; women as well as men".
11 Cf. Nina Witoszek on "Pastoral Enlightenment" and the lack of "Jacobinism"; cf. "Fugitives from Utopia: The Scandinavian Enlightenment Reconsidered", in Sørensen and Stråth, eds., *The Cultural Construction of Norden*, Scandinavian University Press, Oslo/Oxford 1997, pp. 72–90.

The Nordic welfare state: Challenges abound

Today, the Nordic welfare state is challenged from several sides, e.g. demographically and economically. People live longer, and many of them need assistance as they grow old. Recessions in the international economy may affect us. Increased immigration may result in higher expenditure than income and in lower wages for unskilled workers.[12] Neoliberal tendencies will strengthen privatization and lead to greater economic disparities and decreased job security.

Internationally, a globalized and technology-based capitalism is dominating. Here the four freedoms rule: the free movement of goods, services, persons, and capital. Then, the "principle of hydrodynamic" rules as well: jobs and capital move to where expenditure is the lowest and profit the greatest, and workers and immigrants go where wages are higher and the social benefits are the best. (Water does not flow upwards.) In other words, differences between countries are levelled out. Competition rules. Hence, there is a constant need for innovation and growth (economically speaking); hence, there is a constant need for new technology, and with new technology, we are likely to lose jobs. Social disparities start to build, also in Europe.

What of the "Norwegian model", in the midst of all this? What of the Nordic welfare state? Notes of concern abound, as do government-commissioned reports.[13] But they primarily deal with the present and the recent past, not the future. The perspective on the future is often short-term.[14] And for now, we have the oil. And so far, the prices of our export articles have been high, while import prices have been low. But further down the road? In the future, it is often repeated, we must go in for education and innovation.

But we know that crises will come, not the least for ecological reasons. We don't know when, we don't know how, but we do know that it will come. We are seeing it already: climate change and socio-economic tensions, bombed-out states and sectarian wars, political disorientation, and extensive migrations. How much can the welfare state take? Moreover, it is difficult to see how the two systems can at all be compatible: a universal and generous welfare state, and a global technology-based capitalism based on the four liberties. True enough, we get used to phased adjustments – privatization and competitive tendering, labour migration and outsourcing of workplaces, fewer jobs for unskilled workers, and more young people

---

12 As discussed in, e.g., Erling Holmøy and Birger Strøm, "Makroøkonomi og offentlige finanser i ulike scenarioer for innvandring", Statistisk sentralbyrå, *Rapport 15/2012*.

13 Cf. the preparatory legal reports by the Brochmann-committee *NOU 17/2011* and Holden III *NOU 13/2013*.

14 With a certain exception: an interesting report produced by the Fafo Institute addresses the future prospects of the Nordic welfare state towards 2030: *NordMod2030, Fafo-Report 2015–07, "The Nordic model towards 2030. A new chapter?"*

62 Religion and modern institutions

depending on social security. And for now, we can afford a generous welfare state. But in the long run, with increased internationalization and the dismantling of borders,[15] we are headed towards a global equilibrium of wages and working conditions, increased social tensions, and deteriorated living conditions for large population groups, particularly for unskilled workers, and specifically for those who fall outside the labour market.[16] "It is simply impossible to have open borders and at the same time maintain a generous welfare state".[17]

Can the welfare state be saved? In order to provide an honest answer, we must *inter alia* take seriously the challenges posed by a globalized and technology-based capitalism, and take precautionary measures with regard to the ecological challenges. If so, what might a sustainable welfare state look like, under such difficult circumstances? What must be done with regard to the cost of living? How high, how low? And what about the borders? What should we do in order to protect the legal borders of a generous welfare state? Two measures might be considered: (i) reduce material consumption – both in order to meet the ecological challenges and in order to reduce the pressure posed by the four liberties of capitalism, and (ii) protect state borders and national sovereignty[18] from the pressure from a globalized capitalism and international statutes that weaken the state and strengthen the power of capital. Such measures could be considered in defence of a sober Nordic welfare state, where the basic components are moderation and borders.[19]

---

15 In Norway, e.g., with the EEA free trade agreement, that brings Iceland, Lichtenstein and Norway, the EEA countries, into the EU's internal market. An important aspect of this agreement is the so-called investor-to-state dispute settlement, where corporations may sue the state in cases where governmental decisions affect the corporation's profits.

16 Here, new technology plays a crucial part, e.g., through computerization which may lead to fewer jobs. Cf. Frey and Osborne 2013 ("The Future of Employment: How Susceptible are Jobs to Computerisation?"). Reviewing 702 occupations (in the U.S.), Frey and Osborne estimate that 47% are in danger of disappearing due to new technology. Likewise, cf. "Computerization and the Future of Jobs in Norway", by Mika Pajarinen, Petri Rouvinen, and Anders Ekeland; they estimate that around one-third of existing Norwegian jobs will be gone in the next 10–20 years. (ETLA – Muistio, ETLA Brief 34; 22.04.2015).

17 Jeffrey Sachs in an interview with the Danish newspaper *Politiken*, 25 June 2015.

18 There is no doubt that we need international agreements. This concerns trade and travel, it concerns climate and other ecological challenges, and it concerns security. And one might, on a general level, argue for the need for supranational institutions and regulations that might check an otherwise incontrollable capitalism. This is important, not the least for ecological reasons. The challenge is, therefore, on a case-by-case basis, to establish a more sensible balance between national sovereignty and international regulations.

19 Cf. Gunnar Skirbekk, «*Ideen om ein velferdsstat under vanskelege vilkår*» [The Idea of a Welfare State under Difficult Conditions], *Røyst*, Bergen 2015. Earlier version: Gunnar Skirbekk, "The Idea of a Welfare State in a Future Scenario of Great Scarcity", in *The*

This will in the long run pose fundamental challenges for welfare schemes of a Nordic kind. Globally, there is an over-consumption, and globally, there is an over-population that simply is not sustainable. In addition, our technology-based civilization is in many ways uncertain and vulnerable, which might lead to serious international crises.[20] Moreover, nature itself is not to be trifled with; natural disasters and climate changes may have fatal consequences. So, challenges abound, for the welfare state as for anyone. But our main question in this chapter is whether multiculturalism poses a challenge to the welfare state. What, then, do we understand by "multiculturalism"?[21]

Multiculturalism and welfare state – four conceptual points

As noted earlier, here, the terms will be interpreted from a theory-of-science perspective, focusing on four core issues: (a) There is often a *close connection* between *societal institutions* and *cultural identity*. To the extent that the Nordic welfare state as an institution depends on certain socio-cultural preconditions, multiculturalism, in any workable sense, must adapt to these preconditions. (b) To the extent that the Nordic welfare state is a modern *science-based society*, there will be a pluralism of disciplinary perspectives and institutional differentiations, and hence, a "cultural diversity" – in other words, a specific kind of "multiculturalism".[22] (c) In a modern science-based society, *religious arguments* must be purged through enlightened discussions before they can be added weight. This particularly applies to the scripture-based monotheistic religions which, through their validity claims about the supposedly correct understanding of their Holy Scriptures and their conception of God, are open to interpretation and argumentation and therefore also open to enlightenment and modernization. (d) When considering whether certain forms of multiculturalism are compatible with a Nordic welfare state, it makes a difference whether we

---

Rationality of the Welfare State, eds. Erik Oddvar Eriksen and Jørn Loftager, Scandinavian University Press, Oslo 1996, pp. 28–54.

20 Cf. *NOU 24/2000*.

21 Cf. Gunnar Skirbekk, «Kva forstår vi med eit fleirkulturelt samfunn?» [What do we understand by a multicultural society?], *Syn og Segn*, 105/4 1998, pp. 286–313; also in Skirbekk, *Undringa*, Universitetsforlaget, Oslo 2002, pp. 154–186. It is understandable that multiculturalism is often associated with immigration. But we may have multiculturalism without immigration (cf. Lebanon), and immigration without multiculturalism (such as when Swedes move just across the border to Eastern Norway). Furthermore, modern societies, characterized by the differentiation of roles and institutions and pluralistic value systems, may be referred to as "multicultural" regardless of immigration.

22 At the same time, there will be a need for common legal and political institutions, along with a realization that we, as fallible persons, depend on learning from the sciences and from each other and that we therefore need education and enlightenment and a public formation of opinions.

64 Religion and modern institutions

are operating with a *short-term* or a *long-term* perspective, and whether we assume that the future will be *peaceful and harmonic* rather than taking into consideration that serious *crises and conflict* may occur *in the long run*.

(a) *Cultural identities and societal institutions*

Simply put, multiculturalism may refer to the prevalence of several cultures in one society. But 'culture' may itself refer to different things. Some forms of culture may be freely chosen, while others are fixed through their anchoring in traditions and institutions – for instance, certain kinds of attitudes and cultural identities are functional in given institutions, while others are not. Different kinds of attitudes and cultural identities will be more functional in a society where legal and political institutions are well-functioning and relatively incorrupt than they would in societies that lack these kinds of institutions.[23] Culture of this kind is not a detached entity, neither as a personal choice nor as a part of cultural traditions exempt from societal institutions. Culture of this kind is functionally connected to specific institutions and their specific historical learning processes.

It would be a conceptual fallacy to consider this kind of cultural identity as worthy of extraordinary protection regardless of the institutional and socio-political context it belongs to in a functional sense. It would therefore be a mistake to constitutionalize the protection of "cultural identity"[24] as if "culture" is always positive,[25] and as if all forms of cultural identity can be included in modern welfare states, founded on popular enlightenment and public institutions and on a general solidarity.

There are, of course, transitions and grey zones between institution-bound and free-floating forms of culture and cultural identity. But in an institutionally differentiated welfare state, any workable form of

23 This applies to, e.g., forms of loyalty and perceptions of honour, cf. Lebanon in contrast to Scandinavia.
24 Cf. the report delivered to the presidency of the Norwegian Parliament (the *Storting*) by the Human Rights Committee on 19 December 2011 (recommendation for amendment to the Constitution's Article 107); p. 16: "It is the duty of the State to respect the individual's cultural identity [...]" p. 207 (35.2.3.2): "When it comes *immigrants*, the Committee emphasises that the States shall be particularly concerned with the protection of their cultural identity and language, religion, and folklore, [...]". But the relationship between culture and societal circumstances is not addressed. And culture is exclusively referred to in positive terms, p. 207: "Culture creates and reflects values of what one considers a good life [...]". Hm, is that always so?
25 It is not the case that everything an anthropologist might refer to as 'culture' is positive and worthy of protection. This applies not only to extreme cases such as genital mutilation, violence towards children, and contempt for women, but to a range of other issues such as repressive tribal mentality or superstition and premodern attitudes.

multiculturalism would have to adapt to this distinction, although it is in practice a gradualistic one. In concrete terms, this means that, e.g., persons from societies that do not have such institutions, and who settle in societies with such institutions, would have to change and adapt their cultural identity accordingly. They have to configure and reconfigure themselves, to use the digital jargon of today. Any other approach would be unfortunate, also for the persons in question, and moreover, it would be a category mistake.[26]

In short, there are functional institutional limits to how multicultural a given society may become. The question of where to draw the lines will often be a controversial one, but not the claim that such (albeit gradualist) lines exist, nor the claim that there are times when this point will have important practical relevance. For instance, in the case of the functional cultural identity in countries with no well-functioning state institutions (cf. the visit to Beirut). But the point is a general one.

(b) *Science-based societies: a special cultural diversity*

Modern knowledge-societies are science-based. And there is not only one science, but several – a pluralism of scientific and scholarly disciplines and sub-disciplines. This is the case in the university sphere, but also in society at large, where scientific insights and competence are part of various kinds of professions and technologies.

Different sciences operate in interchanging ways with different concepts and methods, within different traditions and institutions.[27] In 1959, C. P. Snow talked about "the two cultures".[28] With today's ongoing specialization and differentiation, we now have a pluralism of science-based "cultures," each with their terminology, their methods and approaches, and their paradigms – in short, a modern form of "multiculturalism".

This point is relevant for our discussion of the welfare state, at two levels: (i) As soon as we attempt to define the welfare state, this problem hits us smack in the face (cf. the introductory remarks earlier): It makes a difference whether we see the welfare state from the point of view of political science and economics or whether we see it in a historical perspective through the theory of science. (ii) Without the sciences, the welfare state cannot prevail: The Nordic welfare state presupposes a science-based society, whether we are thinking of the economy and the

---

26 Backgammon and chess are two different games. Therefore, we cannot interchange the concepts connected to them: In backgammon, there is no queen that needs defending, neither is checkmate possible. Speaking of checkmate in backgammon would be a category mistake.

27 The world looks different for an economist working with game theory than it does for a biologically trained ecologist or a cultural sociologist. It is not merely a matter of what they see and don't see but also of the kinds of values they are attentive towards (or not attentive towards).

28 The natural sciences and the humanities, cf. C. P. Snow, *The Two Cultures and the Scientific Revolution*, Cambridge University Press, Cambridge, 1959.

66 Religion and modern institutions

workforce or the modern political administration. A pluralism of modern sciences (and technologies) is a fundamental precondition for the Nordic welfare state.[29] In this sense, there is a positive relationship between such a science-related "multiculturalism" and a modern Nordic welfare state.[30]

This scientific diversity does not only apply to the causal-explanatory disciplines that may have an instrumental function but also to the interpretative disciplines, such as legal scholarship and the humanities. Moreover, precisely because we are faced with so many disciplinary perspectives, it becomes important to be able to reflect on this pluralism with a view as to which disciplinary perspective is the most appropriate and desirable in any given situation.[31] In addition, in our scientific and scholarly practice, we must be willing to listen to others and be open to counterarguments.

Reflection, doubt, and reasonable discussion thus constitute a common ethos, throughout this "multicultural" pluralism. Furthermore, in a modern knowledge-society, these are virtues that follow along with science-based activities in professional life and in everyday life, far beyond the realm of research communities. And in democratic societies, which are founded on the ideal of enlightened individuals with the ability to form opinions in a reasonable manner, every citizen should (ideally) try to live up to these virtues.[32]

This means that a modern Nordic welfare state should, to the extent that it is science-based and democratic, be open to this science-related "multiculturalism" in a reflecting and discursive manner. But at the same time, this implies that other forms of "multiculturalism", not the least those that have their roots in premodern traditions, will be subjected to criticism. The scripture-based monotheistic religions here hold a special position because they claim to carry valid conceptions of how their Holy

---

29 This is why a theory-of-science perspective is relevant if we want to grasp the particular processes of modernization that lead to the Norwegian version of the Nordic welfare state, cf Skirbekk, "Processes of Modernisation. Scandianvian Experiences", *Transcultural Studies*, 2018; also *Multiple Modernities*, 2011.

30 At the same time, modern science-based and institutionally differentiated societies are problematic in several ways, from the risk of "loss of meaning" ("disenchantment of the world") and the disintegration of our "lifeworld" (with existential rootlessness and the need for lifestyle-related identity markers and religions), to the dissemination of different kinds of technological means of destruction (including nuclear, biochemical, and chemical weapons), and the lack of ecological sustainability.

31 Or, in more negative terms, it becomes important to try to avoid that certain disciplinary perspectives or certain expert groups are allowed to dominate at the expense of other relevant disciplinary perspectives (that is, if we want to have a less one-sided and more sensible take on the issues we are discussing). Cf. Skirbekk 2011.

32 On the notion of citizenship, cf. Silje Aambø Langvatn, *The Idea and Ideal of Public Reason*, University of Bergen, Bergen 2013.

Scriptures and their own monotheistic conceptions of God should be understood, and therefore, these religions are, for inherent (epistemic) reasons, open for the kind of critique of religion that was introduced in the Age of Enlightenment.[33] In short, they are, for inherent reasons, open to a "modernization of consciousness".[34]

(c) *Religious justification of cultural utterances?*

The transition between culture and religion is fluid, partly because these are phenomena that look different depending on the perspective from which they are seen.[35] Moreover, it is well-known that multiculturalism is often understood in religious terms. At the same time, religion, like culture, is often seen as fundamentally connected to identity.[36] And to the extent that a critique of multiculturalism is perceived as a demand that one renounces one's own religion, resistance is understandable. In this regard, I want to note three points:

(i) Religion is not an unequivocal concept (as we have seen in previous chapters). The word may have several meanings, from different and often contradictory versions of the three monotheistic religions, to New Age, satanism, and witch-belief in old and newer versions, not to mention other world religions and different forms of religious practices with or without faith in a deity and theological theses: is there one God, or are there several, or none; is God benevolent, or evil or both? In short, the word alone is today equivocal to the extent that it needs to be interpreted and specified.[37] This semantic point is rich in implications: To claim that something is "religious", may, in itself, not function as an argument for special respect or acknowledgement, neither socially nor legally. First, we must clarify what we mean, and next, we need to be

---

33 As observed earlier in this book.

34 Again, cf. Habermas, *Zwischen Naturalismus und Religion*, 2005, p. 146; English translation 2008. *Between Naturalism and Religion*, p. 136.

35 In religious scholarship, religion is (for methodological reasons) *culture*. For the religious individual (including the religious theologian), religion (their own, at least) is more than culture.

36 In financial conflicts of interests, we can negotiate a compromise by finding a middle ground. Cultural conflicts are normally more complicated, but here, mutual processes of learning may untangle the knot. To some extent, the same can occur between religions, notably given that one does not have an essentialist take on religion. (The same will apply to culture.) But in the monotheistic religions, there are theological theses, e.g. about God being one or about God being three different persons in one, and in such doctrinal conflicts, it is hard to reach a middle ground, for instance the perception that God could be two persons. Precisely for this reason, self-critical critique of religion is important (not as rejection but as purging – again, cf. Kant's criticism of practical reason, where the intention is not to reject but formatively to 'clarify' practical reason).

37 Or be clarified based on the context.

68 Religion and modern institutions

able, in each case, to prove, through arguments that are universally understandable and convincing, that this specific kind of religion deserves respect and acknowledgement.[38] In other words, it is meaningless, for semantic reasons, to treat everything that is referred to as "religion" equally, e.g. in relation to the discussion on multiculturalism. Equal treatment would only make sense in the case that everything that were referred to as "religion" had significant (and positive as well as specific) characteristics in common, but that is hardly the case.[39]

(ii) A lot of what is referred to as religion lies beyond science and reason. But when it, e.g., comes to the scripture-based monotheistic religions, the situation is somewhat different because these religions (among several other things) claim to have valid conceptions of their own Holy Scriptures and of their own monotheistic conceptions of God. This is precisely why these religions, for internal reasons, are open to discussion and argumentation in defence of their own conceptions, and therefore they are, based on their own terms, open to enlightenment and internal modernization. In this sense, we are talking about a critique in a Kantian sense, not as rejection, but as (formative) clarification, and in that sense, this kind of critique does not mean that religious persons must break with their religion – quite the opposite, we are talking about a truer conception of what this religion is all about, and what it requires from religious persons.[40] This is the implication of Habermas' threefold thesis on a "modernization of consciousness": (a) an acknowledgement that there is a religious pluralism and that other people have other religious (and secular) perceptions,[41] (b) an acknowledgement that scientific and scholarly insights and methods must be respected but in a critical manner, and (c) an institutional differentiation between religion and the legal and political systems.

(iii) Religions that have been 'purged' in this sense, will not come into conflict with a modern science-based society.[42] Neither is there any

---

38 In this context, it is interesting to observe that the argumentative defence of hijab has largely been a secular one. Cf. Alexa Døving, «Religionens omveier – det sekulære argument i hijabdebattene», in Sindre Bangstad, Oddbjørn Leirvik and Ingvill Thorson Plesner, eds., *Sekularisme – med norske briller*, Unipub, Oslo 2012.

39 In other words: the question of what religion is, is a matter of definition, i.e. it is a matter of who (in a given context) has the right (and power) to define what should be referred to as religion (potentially for others as well).

40 Cf. the critique of religion in Peter Rohs, *Der Platz zum Glauben*, Mentis Verlag, Münster 2013.

41 Cf. the discussion on "reasonable comprehensive doctrines" and "reasonable disagreement" in Rawls 1993, 58f.

42 Cf., e.g., contributions from Jürgen Habermas, John Rawls, Charles Taylor and Talal Asad, in Talal Asad, Wendy Brown, Judith Butler, Saba Mahmood, publ., *Is Critique Secular? Blasphemy, Injury, and Free Speech*, University of California Press, Berkeley 2009; cf.

inherent reason why religions that have been thus purged would come into conflict with a science-based Nordic welfare state. In this context, it is worth adding a reminder of how religion – in Norway: a Danico-Norwegian variant of Lutheran Protestantism – played a part in the historical processes that eventually resulted in this welfare state. In short, from the early eighteenth century and far into the nineteenth century, this religion had a decisive impact as a state institution emphasizing enlightenment and top-down disciplinary power,[43] and as an inspiration for popular movements with their emphasis on 'people's enlightenment' (*folkeopplysning*) and bottom-up self-organization. This contentious interplay between university-educated state officials and engaged and enlightened laypeople made up a fundamental dynamic in the socio-cultural processes of modernization that led to parliamentarism, and that paved the ground for what would later become the welfare state.[44] In short, while Norwegian Protestantism was an important prerequisite for the welfare state,[45] it also knew how to adjust to a modern science-based society. There is something to be learned here for those who want a Nordic welfare state and also wish to break with religion – but also for those who want a Nordic welfare state but do not wish to break with religion.

(d) *A long-term, crisis-aware perspective*

At the moment, for those of us living in an oil-fuelled welfare state, the situation is reasonably positive and harmonious, also when it comes to the challenges of multiculturalism. We have financial resources; the political support for the welfare state seems unison,[46] and the socio-cultural tensions are manageable. But if we are of the opinion that the welfare state is worthy of preservation, we should work from a long-term and crisis-aware perspective, *inter alia* with regard to the potential challenges that multiculturalism may pose under less favourable conditions than we are currently experiencing.

Habermas, *Zwischen Naturalismus und Religion*, 2005, and contribution in Eduardo Mendieta and Jonathan VanAntwerpen, publ., *The Power of Religion in the Public Sphere*, Columbia University Press, New York 2011, but particularly Rohs, *Der Platz zum Glauben*, 2013. See the text on Habermas in this book.

43 Cf. confirmation and public training in literacy.

44 At the same time, a practical adjustment occurred within Norwegian Protestantism in response to the practical political reality. For example: (i) After the implementation of parliamentarism, the Low Church movement supported a common basic education for all, not for religious reasons, but as a cultural-political strategy against class-division and towards an egalitarian and inclusive national state. (ii) As the state was in the process of developing public welfare institutions, several Christian welfare organisations cooperated by trustingly leaving their projects in the hands of the state.

45 Cf. confirmation and training in literacy which informed popular movements from the time of Hans Nielsen Hauge and beyond.

46 Despite differing views on financing and distribution.

70 Religion and modern institutions

In short, one scenario may look like this: Climate change leads to ecological crisis with conflicts and increasing impediments to access to vital resources (e.g. water and food) in areas with demographic growth. This coincides with an international financial recession and political instability. The same technology that we depend on also makes us vulnerable, e.g. for terror and sabotage, from individuals or groups. In a crisis situation, conflicts will intensify, and this may radicalize the latent multicultural tensions within as well as between states.

How will the welfare state prevail under such circumstances? What about the economy? (Will we be able to adjust to a more frugal approach?[47]) What about political support? And what about multicultural tensions?

It seems sensible to say that a change in attitudes and in political rhetoric is necessary – less short-term and self-complacent, more long term and crisis aware. But in a democracy, the political parties are primarily rigged towards the next election. Future generations do not hold any strong institutional voice. Neither are they visible. No photos in the daily press or on the TV screen. The time perspective is a short one.

Nevertheless, there are things we could and should do with regard to the relationship between the welfare state and multiculturalism in a long-term and crisis-aware perspective. First, it is important to maintain solidarity in work and education policy, and thus reduce the kind of social unrest that nurtures the radicalization of multicultural tensions.[48] Second, it is important to counteract the social forces that turn multiculturalism into a matter of parallel societies,[49] such as group identifiers, withdrawal from social arenas, and resistance towards marriage across cultures.[50] Third, it is important to

---

47 Cf. again, Gunnar Skirbekk, «Ideen om ein velferdsstat under vanskelege vilkår», *Røyst*, Bergen 2015. Earlier version: Gunnar Skirbekk, "The Idea of a Welfare State in a Future Scenario of Great Scarcity", in *The Rationality of the Welfare State*, eds. Erik Oddvar Eriksen and Jørn Loftager, Scandinavian University Press, Oslo 1996, pp. 28–54.

48 This would, so to speak, amount to employing traditional welfare policy in order to preserve a welfare policy for the future.

49 Parallel societies are in themselves problematic, but it is a particularly critical issue in the case that prominent parallel societies have a stronger demographic growth than the general society, and particularly in the case of (financial or ecological) crises that may spark conflict.

50 Here we turn to sociology; cf., e.g., Gilles Kepel (Gilles Kepel, *Banlieue de la République*, Paris, Gallimard 2012) and his analyses of Islamic parallel societies in the socially challenged communities at the outskirts of Paris. These areas, according to Kepel, are characterized by a combination of symbolic markers (which distinguishes an individual from others, from the infidels and the lapsed, and which open for a strict social control within these communities), boycott of common meals (based in a religious justification through an extended conception of halal), and a prohibition of marriage to non-Muslims. Thus, two important institutions for integration in the French society are eliminated; to put it bluntly, the table and the bed – mutual socialization and mutual children across ethnic and religious demarcation lines.

Multiculturalism and the welfare state? **71**

maintain the enlightenment ideal in modern science-based societies, *inter alia* through the internal critique of religion, directed in particular towards unsustainable arguments advocating segregation[51] (e.g. promulgating symbolic group markers and social as well as sexual segregation[52]) and generally with regard to enlightenment and cultural modernization[53] (which will be necessary if we are to be able to meet ecological, demographical, economical, and technological challenges in the future in a civilized manner).

Multiculturalism in modern vulnerable societies

The four points made earlier hold relevance for the discussion of the extraordinary legal protection of minorities in different modern societies within their specific processes of modernization: (i) Our understanding of culture is often connected to certain institutions and historical learning processes. (ii) Modern science-based societies require culture (in a sociological sense) to adjust to institutional differentiations pertinent to such societies and for culture to be enlightened in the form of reflexivity and a general orientation towards the sciences (cf. "the modernization of consciousness"). (iii) In modern science-based societies, there is a basis for self-critical critique of religion, not the least when it comes to scripture-based monotheistic religions. (iv) A realistic and responsible take on the future must consider potential crises and conflicts; based on the precautionary principle, we should, *inter alia*, maintain a critical attitude towards unfortunate symbolic group markers and segregating ways of life.

The question about what is passable (and not passable) in a given modern and science-based society must be considered in the light of these four points. This also applies to modern welfare states. In short, the discussion on multiculturalism should relate to these points with regard to the *universal* requirements of modern societies, with regard to *specific* institutions and learning processes in each modern society, and with regard to a crisis- and conflict-aware *future-time perspective*. For instance, public debates on radicalization in Islamic youth communities, on symbolic group markers such as

---

51 Cf. the argumentation on unintended blasphemy in Chapter 2 in this volume, "To speak of God in the light of the problem of evil. On the need for theology and the danger of unintended blasphemy".

52 This is the political backdrop of the political debate on hijab and halal, but the point is a general one.

53 Cf. e.g. Talal Asad (in Talal Asad et al. publ., *Is Critique Secular? Blasphemy, Injury, and Free Speech*, University of California Press, Berkeley 2009) who argues from a perspective of social anthropology, but based on an essentialist view on culture (religion), and without self-reflection regarding his own validity claims and without addressing the Islam's internal validity claims (on scriptures and on the conception of God, which, for internal reasons require further argumentation, cf., e.g., Chapter 2 in this volume, "To speak of God in the light of the problem of evil. On the need for theology and the danger of unintended blasphemy").

72 Religion and modern institutions

hijab and niqab,[54] or about religious schools and halal food in prisons, should pay heed to these four points.

The Nordic welfare state and socio-cultural preconditions

It is reasonable to assume that the Nordic welfare state, understood as a "model", is based on socio-cultural historic preconditions. But is it reasonable to claim that the welfare state would be able to function as it does today without these historical preconditions? Or are these preconditions integrated into today's Nordic welfare states as underlying conditions?

If we hold that these preconditions are still important and impact a functioning Nordic welfare state, we should pay heed to these socio-cultural conditions, if we are interested in protecting and preserving this welfare state. This applies to democratic participation and self-organization, to 'popular enlightenment' and universal education, to the willingness to follow laws, and to the trust in other actors. It includes learning processes where socio-cultural tensions are reduced and integrated into a national community. In short, it involves an ideal of individual autonomy and general solidarity.

Conversely, if anyone holds that these preconditions are no longer important or no longer impact the welfare state as an organizational model, then the onus is on them to prove this because the stakes are high. Personally, I cannot see that any good arguments have been produced for such a view. But if this were the case, we would be left with a different and meagre conception compared to what constituted the basis for the Nordic welfare state. And if this were the case, we would have less solid ground from which to defend the Nordic welfare state in the face of future potential challenges of multiculturalism, potentially with premodern features, far from ideals of individual autonomy and general solidarity, and far from the Nordic experiences connected to self-organizing and enlightened participation in the public formation of opinions and in political struggles.

The precautionary principle is crucial for a responsible policy concerning ecological challenges; the same can be said with regard to the socio-cultural challenges that the Nordic welfare state is facing.

Don't get me wrong: The Nordic welfare state does not require everyone to be the same. In our society, there have always been counter- and multicultural tensions, and in modern societies, there will always be disagreements

---

54 An example, as food for thought: cf. Bo Lidegaard's book *Countrymen. How Denmark's Jews Escaped the Nazis*, London, Atlantis Books 2015; Lidegaard refers to the great majority of Danish Jews being salvaged during World War II because they were considered "fellow countrymen": they did not live in segregated communities; rather, they were well-integrated into Danish society, as opposed to what happened in Hitler's Germany, where the Jews were gradually segregated and marked by the Star of David on their coats. Few were salvaged. Few survived.

and conflicts of interest. But neither is it satisfactory to restrict the matter to a case of a detached organizational model and egocentric self-interest. The welfare state has its historical and socio-cultural preconditions, which function as prerequisites for a community. If we want to take part in the benefits administered by this community, we would be wise to respect these preconditions – and in these historical learning processes, "religion" is included, not in an abstract sense but in different local and specific variations.

PART IV

Religion in modern societies

6

RELIGION AS SOCIAL INTEGRATION

Jürgen Habermas

Religion in secular societies

It caused quite a stir when Jürgen Habermas, at an advanced age – after an extraordinarily extensive and varied writing career – in several publications emphasized religion as a positive resource in modern societies, opposing the thesis that religion has lost its relevance in secular societies. This view is clearly expressed in the collections *Zwischen Naturalismus und Religion*[1] (*Between Naturalism and Religion*,[2] 2005) and *Nachmetaphysisches Denken II*[3] (*Postmetaphysical Thinking II*,[4] 2012), and most recently, the two volumes that together constitute *Auch eine Geschichte der Philosophie*[5] (*Also a History of Philosophy*[6]) from 2019, an *oeuvre* of more than 1,700 pages, about the development of the relationship between "faith" and "knowledge" (*Glauben und Wissen*), presented as a historical learning process, with a particular focus on the interplay between Western Christianity and philosophy.

As a philosopher, Habermas is a secularist, also with regard to science and the rule of law.[7] At the same time, he advocates for religious individuals' right

---

1 Suhrkamp, Fr.a.M. 2005.
2 English translation by Ciaran Cronin. Polity Press, Cambridge 2008.
3 Suhrkamp, Fr.a.M. 2012.
4 English translation by Ciaran Cronin. Polity Press, Cambridge 2017.
5 Suhrkamp, Berlin 2019.
6 To be published by Polity Press in three volumes, the first volume in the autumn of 2023.
7 He refers to himself as a "religiously tone-deaf citizen"; cf. English translation, *Between Naturalism and Religion*, Polity Press, Cambridge 2008. p. 112 ("religiös unmusikalische [r] Bürger"), cf. Habermas, *Zwischen Naturalismus und Religion*, Suhrkamp, Fr.a.M. 2005, p. 118. At the same time, he talks about "post secular" societies: institutionally secular societies, where religion nevertheless plays a role in society, cf. same source, English translation p. 111; original

DOI: 10.4324/9781003441618-10

78 Religion in modern societies

to participate in the public discourse, not only for their own sake, as an anti-discriminatory measure but also, and not the least, because Habermas holds that religious experiences and religious language can contain important insights, insights that all parties would benefit from having "translated" and transferred to a generally accessible language, accessible regardless of religion and worldview.

The crux of the matter is this: What is it, precisely, that may *be lost* if "religious truths" are not heard in the public discourse in modern science-based and institutionally differentiated societies? And what might it mean, more precisely, that religious insights ("truths"[8]) become *"translated"* to a profane language and made accessible also for non-religious citizens?

These are the kinds of issues that Habermas tentatively addresses in his work *Auch eine Geschichte der Philosophie* by reviewing the history of how fundamental discussions (particularly in the Western world) have led to a differentiation between "faith" and "knowledge"[9] but also to communicative "translations" between them, as Habermas sees it.

This point, about the interplay between differentiation and mediation, corresponds to a basic feature of the "dialectics of modernity": to the extent that modernization is characterized by *differentiation*, institutionally and epistemically,[10] a need simultaneously emerges for a certain *balancing* or *mediation* between the institutions and validity spheres that have been thus separated.[11] From this perspective, with a view to the differentiation between "faith" and "knowledge" in Western modernization, Habermas is concerned with mediating "translations" of valuable religious experiences into a non-religious language.[12]

---

version p. 116, with reference to Klaus Eder, "Europäische Säkularisierung – ein Sonderweg in die postsäkulare Gesellschaft?", *Berliner Journal für Soziologie*, 3, 2002, pp. 331–343.

8 Habermas uses the word *Wahrheit* ("truth") in this context. Cf. Habermas 2005, pp. 137–138 /English translation 2008, pp. 131–132, where he uses the expression *Wahrheitsgehalt* ("truth content") several times in relation to religious utterances and religious contributions ("Wahrheitsgehalte von religiösen Äußerungen" and "Wahrheitsgehalt religiöser Beiträge"), and p. 147 /English translation p. 140, where he speaks of "religious truths" ("religiöse Wahrheiten").

9 Either from a religious point of departure, as in Martin Luther (who at some level differentiates between "faith" and "knowledge", in defence of religion), or from a secularist point of departure, as in the logical positivists in the inter-war period (who distinguish between religious and scientific language in rejecting the religious language as cognitively meaningless).

10 Cf. the take on modernization in Max Weber: modernization as rationalization and differentiation of institutions and "value spheres".

11 For instance, between state, market, and lifeworld (as differentiated societal institutions) and between different disciplines and forms of knowledge. On the last point, cf. the pressing need for cross-disciplinary and interdisciplinary competence, counteracting one-sided expertise and increasing specialisation in today's society.

12 But the word "translation" requires clarification when that which is to be "translated" are not verbally articulated statements but meaning-laden "horizons" or practice-based experiences. For it is one thing to "translate" between different languages or verbal statements – it is something else to "translate" (or "mediate") *practice-based experiences and insights*. In

The two volumes that constitute *Auch eine Geschichte der Philosophie* make for an impressive *oeuvre*, and for readers, an immensely rich histori-cal-intellectual *bildung* project. Here, we will restrict ourselves to focus on certain central points and topics, with no pretentions of doing justice to the work as a whole.[13] But it may be useful to begin by referring to two topics that have also been central in previous publications (*Zwischen Naturalismus und Religion* from 2005 and *Nachmetaphysisches Denken II* from 2012) – that is, the issues of (i) *motivation of civic solidarity* and of (ii) the role of *ritual* in this context.

The motivation of solidarity – in the books from 2005 and 2012

It is commonly emphasized that it is one thing to *justify* a norm for acts but another to *adhere* to such a norm. It is one thing to acknowledge that a norm is *valid* but another to have the *motivation* to act in accordance with the norm.

But there are exceptions. If it can be proven that certain norms are neces-sary for serious discussions, then we must adhere to these norms when we argue. This also applies when we try to argue that this norm is unnecessary! This is the basic pattern of the main argument of transcendental pragmatics as we find it in the writings of friend and colleague of Jürgen Habermas, Karl-Otto Apel: Normative principles that are *not rejectable* lest we find our-selves in the predicament of *self-referential inconsistency* are inescapable and therefore necessarily valid when we are engaged in discussion.[14]

---

this context, cf. the discussions on so-called tacit knowledge or knowing how in the works of philosophers such as Michael Polanyi and Ludwig Wittgenstein or, in a Norwegian con-text, Kjell S. Johannessen and Yu Zhenhua (who wrote his dissertation on this topic at the University of Bergen). Habermas refers to such "translations" as a "process of assimilation [appropriation]" (which may have the effect of "transforming the original religious mean-ing", cf. Habermas, *Zwischen Naturalismus und Religion*, 2005, p. 115 /English translation 2008, p. 110). He provides an example: the "translation" of the Christian doctrine that all humans are created "in God's image" to "the idea of equal and unconditional *dignity* of *all* human beings" (English translation 2008, p. 110: "The translation of the theological doctrine of creation in God's image into the idea of the equal and unconditional dignity of all human beings constitutes *such a conserving [rettende; 'saving'] translation*"; my italics and parenthesis). (Habermas 2005: "Die Übersetzung der Gottesebenbildlichkeit des Menschen in die gleiche und unbedingt zu achtende Würde aller Menschen ist *eine solche rettende Übersetzung*" (Habermas 2005, pp. 115–116; my italics.)

13 Here it is timely to add a reminder of the essential point for our purposes which concerns what *translation* might mean in this context and also what the word *religion* may signify beyond the theistic and organized world religions. On different concepts of religion, see Habermas, *Nachmetaphysisches Denken II*, 2012, p. 77 /English translation 2017 [chapter 3, "The Intrinsic Meaning of Ritual Behaviour", Para. 1].

14 On this discussion, cf. Gunnar Skirbekk, *Philosophie der Moderne*, Velbrück Wissenschaft, Weilerswist 2017, pp. 18–26.

80 Religion in modern societies

But when we are not engaged in reasonable and serious argumentation, what then? Are we still obliged to adhere to these norms?[15] Well, a lot of our everyday doings are far from such discursive situations, so it would be strange if we should be obliged to adhere to these norms in all and any circumstances. Then again, as autonomous and enlightened citizens in science-based modern societies, which are, at least to some extent, characterized by an enlightenment culture, such norms of argumentation will apply in many contexts, internally in various professions and occupations, and ideally in the general public discourse as well. But there may be different kinds of exceptions to this, e.g. based on the question of what kinds of situations warrant rhetorical manoeuvres that may make us see issues and situations in new and exciting ways.[16]

But beyond this? What makes us *act* morally? What is it that generates a moral *motivation*?[17] This is essentially an *empirical* question to be addressed by different kinds of scientific expertise, as Habermas also emphasizes.[18] At the same time, he notes that the traditional theories of moral philosophy are solid

15 Opposing Apel, concerning the transition from discussion to acts, cf. Habermas, *Zwischen Naturalismus und Religion*, 2005, p. 103: "Er [Apel] will aus der Selbstbesinnung auf die in Argumentationen immer schon vorausgesetzten Normen ohne weitere Vermittlungen die *moralische Verpflichtung … ableiten,…*" [my italics] /English translation 2008, p. 95: "He [Apel] wants to derive from the self-reflection on the norms that are always already presupposed in the argumentation, without further mediation, the *moral obligation …*" [my italics].
16 Cf. the literary language of an existentialist such as Søren Kierkegaard who, simply put, aims to communicate a way of understanding and a way of being rather than factual statements; cf., e.g., Gilje, Nils, and Gunnar Skirbekk. *A History of Western Thought: From Ancient Greece to the Twentieth Century*. Routledge, London 2001. pp. 367–369. Cf. reflection on the need for a religious language in Gunnar Skirbekk, *Den filosofiske uroa*, Universitetsforlaget, Oslo 2005, p. 179 f.
17 Habermas is self-critical with regard to this point, cf. Habermas *Nachmetaphysisches Denken II*, 2012, p. 13:

> Ich bin in der *Theorie des kommunikativen Handelns* [1981] vorschnell von der überinklusiven Annahme ausgegangen, dass sich die *rationale-motivierende Bindungskraft* [my italics] guter Gründe, die für die handlungskoordinierende Funktion sprachlicher Verständigung den Ausschlag gibt, *allgemein* auf die Versprachlichung eines zunächst rituell gesicherten Grundeinverständnisses zurückführen lässt: …

> /English translation 2017 [Under: "Linguistification of the Sacred: In Place of a Preface", Para. 12]:

> In the *Theory of Communicative Action*, I made the rash and overinclusive assumption that the rationally motivating binding force of good reasons, on which the coordinating function of linguistic communication turns, can be traced back in general to the linguistification of a basic agreement initially secured through ritual.

18 Cf. Habermas, *Nachmetaphysisches Denken II*, 2012, p. 132: "Die Philosophie … kann nicht für die kulturellen Überlieferungen und die Sozialisationsprozesse, auch nicht für die Institutionen einstehen, die den moralischen Gesichtspunkt in den Herzen der handelnden Subjekte verankern müssen" /English translation 2017: "But philosophy cannot take responsibility for the cultural traditions and processes of socialization, or for the institutions, that must anchor the moral point of view in the hearts of acting subjects". [In Chapter 5, under: "Why a Secular Translation of Religious Potentials at All?", Para. 5.]

enough to deal with what he refers to as normal cases of problem-solving in well-functioning democracies.[19] "But in times of crisis, when the existing institutions and procedures are no longer able to cope with the pressure of problems, the parameters of the established range of values must first undergo a change"[20]; in that case, a motivation is required that may inform acts of *"socially solidary action"*.[21] It is here that religious tradition, in Habermas' view, may play an important part. In short, Habermas presupposes that complex modern societies are *in crisis*,[22] suffering from "motivational deficiency",[23] and in response to this challenge, he points to religious traditions and practices.[24]

Some brief comments on what has been said so far:

(a) Habermas understands the crisis in complex modern societies primarily as a *normative* crisis, connected to *social integration* and a *motivational deficiency*.[25] But *how accurate* is this? Is it primarily a matter of failing "motivation"? Cf. ardent Trump supporters on the one hand and *ditto* Islamists on the other. There is hardly a lack of motivation in these groups, at least not that one alone. Might it not also be a lack of *knowledge*, and of *enlightenment*, in a complex modern world where many turn to (and believe in) "fake news" and conspiracy theories as simplifying explanations of a complicated and difficult world? And might it not at the same

---

19 In Chapter 5, under: "Why a Secular Translation of Religious Potentials at All?", Para. 6.
20 "Times of crisis", but what kind of crisis? Habermas here refers to eugenics (and human enhancement) driven by financial interests, through the use of modern technology (cf. Habermas 2012, p. 132, footnote 23 /English translation 2017 [in Chapter 5, under: "Why a Secular Translation of Religious Potentials at All?", Para. 6], footnote 25) – a recurring theme in Habermas, cf. *Die Zukunft der menschlichen Natur. Auf dem Weg zu einer liberalen Eugenik*? Suhrkamp, Fr.a.M. 2001 /English translation, *The Future of Human Nature*, Polity Press, Cambridge 2003.
21 Original: «gesellschaftlich solidarische[s] Handeln», cf. Habermas i *Nachmetaphysisches Denken II*, 2012, p. 131. /English translation 2017, in Chapter 5, under: "Why a Secular Translation of Religious Potentials at All?", Para. 5 (author's italics).
22 "Meine Frage ist heute: Reicht das Potential dieser großartigen und, wie ich hoffe, unverlierbaren Aufklärungskultur aus, um unter Bedingungen komplexer Gesellschaften die in Krisesituationen erforderlichen Motive zu gesellschaftlich solidarischem Handeln zu erzeugen", Habermas 2012, p. 131. /English translation 2017,

> The question I want to ask is the following: Is the potential of this admirable and, let us hope, resilient Enlightenment culture sufficient under conditions of rapidly increasing social complexity to motivate the kind of collective action, of action in *social solidarity*, which is required in times of crisis if social movements are to develop?
> [In Chapter 5, under: "Why a Secular Translation of Religious Potentials at All?", Para. 4.]

23 Original, "motivationales Defizit", Habermas 2012, p. 131 /English translation, 2017 [In Chapter 5, under: "Why a Secular Translation of Religious Potentials at All?", Para. 4].
24 "Die religiöse Gemeindepraxis", Habermas 2012, p. 133 / "the practice of religious communities", English translation 2017, in Chapter 5, under: "Why a Secular Translation of Religious Potentials at All?", Para. 6.
25 With "a motivational deficiency" for "solidary actions"; English translation 2017, in Chapter 5, under: "Why a Secular Translation of Religious Potentials at All?", Para. 6. Habermas 2012, p. 132.

82 Religion in modern societies

time be a matter of *institutional* challenges, and also challenges of an epistemic nature, in modern science-based and institutionally differentiated societies,[26] in addition to crises related to *ecology*?

(b) With regard to social integration, Habermas particularly focuses on religion, on *religious practice*, and the *mediation of religious traditions*. But is it merely or primarily "religion" that has and can have such a social-integrative function? Might not other factors be relevant as well, also for the kind of crises where motivation plays a role[27] – for instance, in cases where *certain institutions* presuppose and promote certain roles and ways of life, such as certain kinds of cultural modernization – for instance, the need to live up to the role as autonomous and co-responsible citizens in a modern democracy founded on the rule of law?

(c) Moreover, it is not always clear what it is that Habermas means by the word "religion".[28] For instance, when it is indicated that "religious" practice and mediation of tradition promote motivation of social solidarity, would it not be useful to specify what it is that one has in mind when one uses words like "religion" and "religious" – as not all forms of "religion" might have such a positive impact?[29]

Ritual practice – in the book from 2012

Based on, *inter alia*, the works of developmental psychologist Michael Tomasello,[30] Habermas develops a hypothesis on the developmental-historical role of *ritual actions*. Ritual practices, and hence religious rituals, are understood as important because they generate "normative binding energies".[31] Religious rituals thus appear as a remedy for a "motivational deficiency".[32]

---

26 E.g. as demonstrated in my publication *Epistemic Challenges in the Modern World. From 'Fake News' and 'Post Truth' to Underlying Epistemic Challenges in Science-Based Risk-Societies.* LIT Verlag, Zürich 2019.

27 Depending on how we understand the "crisis" (more on this later).

28 Cf., e.g., *Nachmetaphysisches Denken II*, 2012, p. 77, English translation 2017, [chapter 3, "The Intrinsic Meaning of Ritual Behaviour", Para. 1], on different conceptions of "religion". But the work from 2019 is specifically concerned with Western Christianity.

29 Cf., e.g., Habermas 2012, pp. 131–135, English translation 2017, Chapter 5, section: "Why a Secular Translation of Religious Potentials at All?"

30 Tomasello (along with other developmental psychologists) emphasises the social as a decisive advantage of human evolution (*inter alia* based on experiments on the interaction of young children, in contrast to chimpanzees). Cf. *Nachmetaphysisches Denken II*, 2012, pp. 14–15 and 77–95 /English translation 2017 in Chapter 2 under: "The Lifeworld as a Space of Symbolically Embodied Reasons" and Chapter 3 section V, "Communicating with Someone about Something".

31 Original: "rituelle[] Erzeugung normativer Bindungsenergien", Habermas 2012, p. 17 / English translation 2017, "Linguistification of the Sacred: In Place of a Preface", Para. 7.

32 Habermas 2012, p. 132 /English translation 2017, Chapter 5, under: "Why a Secular Translation of Religious Potentials at All?", Para. 4.

And, Habermas adds, without this, without such ritual practices, today's religions would not be able to assert themselves in the face of secular thought.[33] At the same time, members of religious communities, based on such cultic practices, have access to a source of solidarity[34] which is not, as it were, accessible for the non-religious.[35]

Another novel, and perhaps unexpected, take by Habermas – a philosopher who many associate with argumentative reason, in seminars and in the public sphere! But this is not the first time he surprises us. In many ways, Habermas is a moving target, open to criticism and self-criticism, ready to turn over a new leaf and venture into new problem complexes – from his earlier works on "structural transformation" of the public space, to theory of science and critique of science, epistemologically fuelled interests and critiques of positivism and technocracies, and political theory based on reflections on the relationship between theory and practice – during the student revolt – over to speech act theory and reflections on validity[36] – and later he advocated a position in defence of the legal system and of the rule of law, and the European Union, and, most recently, a defence of religion in modern societies. As a reader, it can be quite an ordeal to keep up!

Again, a few critical comments:

(a) If ritual practices are important because they generate "binding forces" and "motivation", then this would surely apply to all ritual practices. Not solely to ritual practices of a religious nature, but also, e.g., to ritual practices of a political nature. Here, it seems relevant to recall the well-targeted and efficient use of rituals under the auspices of the Nazi regime in Germany,

---

33 "Ohne dieses *proprium* hätten sich die Religionen nicht auf eigensinnige Weise gegenüber dem säkularen Denken bis heute behaupten können". Habermas 2012, p. 78 / "Without this *proper core*, the religions would not have been able to stubbornly affirm their status in contrast to secular thought up to the present day". English translation 2017, in chapter 3, section "A Hypothesis Concerning the Evolutionary Meaning of Rites", Para. 3.

34 But then, we might ask: Solidarity towards whom? Towards everyone, or primarily their own community (as is the case in tribal societies)? And furthermore: Solidarity with those living in the present, or with future generations as well? And what does "solidarity" mean in practice, for instance, with regard to our own "ecological footprint"?

35 Original, quote: "Die Mitglieder religiöser Gemeinschaften können sogar das Privileg für sich beanspruchen, im Vollzug ihrer kultischen Praktiken den Zugang zu einer archaischen Erfahrung – und zu einer Quelle der Solidarität – behalten zu haben, die sich den ungläubigen Söhnen und Töchtern der Moderne verschlossen hat". Habermas 2012, p. 95 / "Religious communities, in performing their rituals, have preserved the access to an archaic experience – and to a source of solidarity – from which the unbelieving sons and daughters of modernity are excluded" (English translation 2017, Chapter 3 VII "The Transformations of the Sacred Complex", Final Para.).

36 So, when Habermas gave a lecture at the University of Bergen in 2014, half of the audience left the room during the break out of pure confusion over what was going on!

84 Religion in modern societies

with music and parades,[37] and with social markers – swastika on armlets and raised right arms – visible markers of who is "with us" and who is not.

(b) This leads us to our next question: Are all "binding forces" and "motivations", generated by rituals, always for the good? Or should we distinguish between ritual practices that have positive effects and ritual practices that have less positive, or perhaps even negative effects? And if so, should this not be considered with regard to ritual practices of a religious nature, as well? If this question is a meaningful one, the implications are important: competent and self-critical critique will then be required, not only towards political practices but also towards practices relevant to religion. In short, then, we need critique of religion, not as rejection, but as Kantian purging.[38]

(c) Moreover, if "binding energies" brought on by rituals are to be "translated" or transferred to others, including those who are not members of the religious community in question, how would this come about? Again, we are here not talking about "translating" verbal statements as we do from one language to another but about communicating practice-based socialization and experience. To what extent is it then the case that the same ritual practices must be practiced and experienced in order for potential recipients to be able to assimilate the content?

Meaning-constitutive horizons – in *Auch eine Geschichte der Philosophie*, **from 2019**

So far, we have noted a few points in the works that have paved the ground for *Auch eine Geschichte der Philosophie*, focusing on *solidary motivation* and *ritual practice*. Against this background, we will now address some central aspects of the comprehensive work from 2019. But first, an introductory remark about the expression *meaning-constitutive horizons*, which in Habermas is understood as the "horizon" *from which* we see and understand, not merely on an individual level, but as a meaning-constitutive and identity-creative precondition for a group or a community.

Habermas also uses the word "world-picture" (Weltbild)[39] – understood as the "picture" *by which* and *through which* we perceive the world and ourselves[40] (and not as a "picture" in front of us, that we look *upon*).[41]

---

37 Playwright Ingmar Bergman experienced these rituals as a young man in Germany in the mid-1930s, and his fascination with Hitler lasted until the war was over. Cf. his autobiography *Laterna Magica*.

38 Cf. the discussion on critique of religion earlier in this publication.

39 E.g. in the heading of part III (Habermas 2019, vol. I, p. 307).

40 Cf. Matthew 7-3: "Why do you look at the speck of sawdust in your brother's eye and pay no attention to the plank in your own eye?". Norwegian philosopher Hans Skjervheim promptly responded: "Because that is what you use to see at all!" (But again, one might also reflect on one's own point of view and one's own preconditions!)

41 But we may (transcendental-philosophically) reflect upon "conditions for possibilities" (Bedingung der Möglichkeit) for our own understanding; cf., e.g., the section on Immanuel

This point resonates with a well-known tradition in the history of philosophy, focusing on intersubjective and historically shifting *horizons of understanding*, represented by words such as *spirit of the age* (*Zeitgeist*) in Hegel, *life-world* in Husserl, and *destiny* (*Geschick*) in Heidegger.[42] In Habermas, in the work from 2019, the development of the relationship between *faith* and *reason*,[43] between religion and philosophy, is a core topic – a development which, according to Habermas, may be conceptualized and discussed as *learning processes*, by *reconstructing* the development of such meaning-constitutive horizons of understanding.[44]

Essential points in the book *Also a History of Philosophy,* **German original from 2019**

Habermas refers to the two volumes as an attempt to grasp the *structural changes of the world-pictures*, in the Western world, as a *learning process*.[45] But why? Why is this important? Because we (as just mentioned) are in *crisis*,[46] for Habermas, primarily a crisis connected to a "motivational deficiency" caused by a lack of "*social integration*".

It is here worth recalling the distinction between "life-world" and "system",[47] as a backdrop for the distinction between "social integration" and "systemic integration":

Systemic integration concerns societal organization of and adaption to natural circumstances.[48] This requires learning that provides useful knowledge about matters of fact.

Kant in Skirbekk/Gilje, *A History of Western Thought: from Ancient Greece to the twentieth century*, Routledge, London 2001.

42 Originals: *Zeitgeist*, *Lebenswelt*, and *Geschick* – as cues for related concepts (concerning historically situated horizons of understanding) in, respectively, Hegel, Husserl, and Heidegger (in Heidegger, dynamically understood as *Welterschließung*, "world disclosure") – to stay within the sphere of these three philosophers ('the three Hs' as they were called, at Sorbonne in the post-war years: *les trois h's*).

43 In German, *Glauben* und *Wissen*, two central words that are included in the subtitles of both volumes.

44 Which, in turn, originates from the identity-constitutive myths and socially integrative ritual practices.

45 Cf., e.g., Habermas 2019, vol. I, p. 136. Moreover, Habermas' first *oeuvre* (1962) was titled "Strukturwandel der Öffentlichkeit" (English translation, *The structural transformation of the public sphere*, MIT Press, 1991), in the book from 2019, the topic is "Strukturwandel der Weltbilder" ("The structural transformation of world-pictures").

46 The theme of crisis encircles the work. It is the basic theme of Chapter 1 in the first volume (pp. 40–74) and in the postscript in volume II (pp. 797–799).

47 Cf. the discussions on system and lifeworld based in *Theorie des kommunikativen Handelns*, Suhrkamp, Fr.a.M. 1981. English translation, *The Theory of Communicative Action*, Beacon Press, Boston 1984.

48 From established trade-relations and simple power structures in historically early communities, via family-based tribal societies, to extensive and complex states. What is needed in order to adapt institutions and infrastructure, is primarily, according to Habermas, instrumental and strategic knowledge.

86 Religion in modern societies

Social integration concerns the societal glue, the "mentality-constitutive force"[49] and the "identity-constitutive world pictures"[50] that may generate solidary motivation and legitimize current institutions and power relations. Hence, social integration may have a stabilizing effect. But because identity-constitutive and motivational world-pictures depend on *faith*, on being perceived as trustworthy and convincing, *crises* may emerge if the world-pictures are *questioned*, *doubted*, or otherwise impaired. In these cases, doubt and a lack of trust may have a destabilizing effect.

These two volumes aim to grasp the "structural changes of the world-pictures" as a "learning process", and in correspondence to sociological perceptions, *religion* is conceived (as a meaning-constitutive "world-picture") *in a social-integrative perspective.*[51]

The objective is to provide a credible reconstruction of the history of Western philosophy (up until Habermas' own position, with communicative and discursive reason), with a focus on the interplay between philosophy and religion, mainly Western Christianity.

A brief outline of the structure of the book *Auch eine Geschichte der Philosophie,* 2019

Early tribal societies: communication-constitutive rites and myths

Homo sapiens were, from the very outset, dependent on the ability to communicate. Language was a crucial factor. But in order to ensure unity in the group, so were rituals. And for the same reason, mythical tales. In short, through rites and myths, humans learned to relate to each other in a communicative way[52] (in addition to relating instrumentally to the surrounding world). Therefore, rites and myths are the "sacred roots" of the subsequent development of social unity and communicative competence (in the "Axial Age"), as Habermas sees it.[53]

---

49 Habermas 2019, vol. II, p. 805.
50 Habermas 2019, vol. I, p. 136.
51 Cf. the role of religion in the works of Émile Durkheim.
52 Here, Habermas draws on development theories and research, e.g. in developmental psychologist Michael Tomasello in the book *Die kulturelle Entwicklung des menschlichen Denkens. Zur Evolution der Kognition* (2002), which Habermas refers to in *Nachmetaphysches Denken II* (2012) pp. 77–95 /English translation 2017, Chapter 3 section V, *Communicating with Someone about Something.* Cf. also the section "Mythos und Ritus" in the work from 2019, vol. I, pp. 201–245 (where Habermas, moreover, argues against what he sees as recent and unfortunate "intentionalistic" and "mentalistic" aspects of Tomasello's book *Eine Naturgeschichte des menschlichen Denkens*, from 2014; cf. Habermas 2019, vol. I, footnote 80, p. 235 and footnote 88, p. 241).
53 Cf. the title of part II in vol. I from 2019: *Die sakralen Wurzeln der achsenzeitlichen Überlieferungen.*

Global "Axial Age" (800–200 B.C.), with a focus on monotheism and Greek philosophy

After World War II, in 1949, Karl Jaspers introduced the thesis of an "Axial Age",[54] of a momentous shift in human self-perception, that occurred almost simultaneously in different places, such as China, India, and in the West – in other words, a global, not a Eurocentric development[55] – driven by religious leaders and philosophers, e.g. Confucius in China and Siddhartha Gautama (Buddha) in India, and by monotheism in the Middle East and by philosophers in Greece. Habermas refers to this thesis on fundamental civilizational shifts in different cultures but focuses primarily on the relationship between Jewish and later Christian monotheism on the one hand, and Greek philosophy, particularly Plato, on the other.[56]

The Medieval Age: Western Christianity and Platonism

In his discussion of the Medieval Age, Habermas follows up with a particular focus on the development in the interplay between Western Christianity and Platonism, in a neo-platonic sense, as in Plotinus and Augustine, up until the addition of Aristotelian philosophy in Thomas Aquinas in the thirteenth century and the subsequent nominalist critique brought forth by, e.g., William Ockham. Central here is the mediation between theology and philosophy, as is the development of the relationship between Church and State, and the Christian conception of Natural Law,[57] in a legal and social-integrative perspective.

Reformation: Luther, and the distinction between "faith" and "reason"

For Habermas, Luther represents a "shift in form" in theology: In contrast to the active assimilation between thought and faith in the Medieval Age, Luther advocates for *distinguishing between* these two and rather focusing on the personal aspects of faith, "faith alone" (*sola fide*)[58]: Each individual answers to God. Legal regulations are thus delimited to external circumstances.[59] But when it comes to the right to object, the right to protest against a tyrannic

---

54 Cf. Karl Jaspers, *Vom Ursprung und Ziel der Geschichte*, 1949 / English translation, *The Origin and Goal of History*, 1953.

55 The debate about an "Axial Age" has been further developed, *inter alia*, by sociologist Shmuel Eisenstadt, who, based on comparative civilization studies, emphasizes that this perspective opens for a conception of "multiple modernities".

56 Cf. Habermas 2019, vol. I, pp. 307–459; specific reference p. 478.

57 *Inter alia* with a focus on the thesis that humans, all humans, are created in the image of God.

58 Faith alone and the scripture alone (*sola scriptura*).

59 Quote from Luther, in Habermas 2019, vol. II, p. 66: "Denn der Glaube ist ein freies Werk, zu dem man niemanden zwingen kann"; faith is based on freedom; nobody can be forced to believe.

88 Religion in modern societies

ruler, Habermas points to an ambiguity in Luther's teachings: On the one hand, the right to object, on the other, secular rulers are said to be appointed by God, and thus they have the right to demand obedience.[60] According to the Aristotelian tradition, rulers should facilitate a good society; for Luther, the task of secular rulers is primarily to counteract the negative.

New sciences: the paradigm shift from God's eye to the thinking subject

Habermas refers to the new experimental and mathematically formulated natural sciences as representing a *paradigm shift*, from a God-based ontology to the individual as a *thinking subject*, and to nature and the surrounding world as *object* in the shape of material elements which move on the basis of *mechanical natural laws* – as in René Descartes (1569–1650), who, based on "methodic doubt"[61] starts with the thinking subject (*res cogitans*), who relates to the objective extended world (*res extensa*), which we can know with certainty because a perfect God would not fool us. In accordance with Descartes, we find the *rationalists*, such as Spinoza and Leibniz. At the same time, we have thinkers who start from the subject's thinking as based on experience in the form of *sensory impressions* – as in John Locke (1632–1704), who saw the human mind as virtually a "clean slate" (*tabula rasa*), which is gradually filled up by sensory impressions from the external world, in addition to *introspections* in one's interiority, which, in turn, are shaped by thought. Corresponding to this, we have the *empiricists*, such as Berkeley and Hume. Preceding this line of thought, was Francis Bacon (1561–1626), with an eye for the practical value of the *instrumental utilization* of the new natural sciences. God is present, in different ways, in most of the philosophers and natural science researchers in this period, but as a "watchmaker" of the world conceived as "clockworks", and not as the God of Abraham and Isaac. With exceptions, such as the philosopher and scientist Blaise Pascal (1623–1662), who emphasized, "The heart has its reasons, which reason does not know",[62] and who regarded religious faith as a (sensible) existential choice.

Hume and Kant: deconstruction and reconstruction of the Christian legacy

Habermas considers Hume an objectivizing sceptic, critical towards religion, and lacking the philosophical resources to justify universally valid normative

---

60 Famous to the point of notoriety is Luther's brutal declaration under the Peasants' Revolt in 1524–1525: "Wider die räuberischen und mörderischen Rotten der Bauern"; cited in Habermas 2019, vol. 2, p. 69.
61 And *cogito ergo sum*, "I think, therefore I am".
62 Blaise Pascal, in the book *Pensées* (*Thoughts*): "*Le coeur a ses raisons que la raison ne connaît point*".

issue related to the need for "motivational resources" which provide "forces for autonomous actions"[73]: Although discourse (and the "unforced force of the better argument") invites a "we-perspective", a "mutual assimilation of perspectives of *all* who may be affected",[74] discourse alone will only leave us with a weak force of motivation. Habermas is looking for stronger "motivational resources" and seeks to find them in religion, with a particular focus on Western Christianity.

Habermas closes the postscript by stating that secular reason has been separated from religious faith.[75] Secular modern society has "for good reasons" turned away from the "the transcendent".[76] Though, he adds: with the "disappearance of thought that transcends the world as a whole", reason itself could "wither away".[77]

When "faith" and "knowledge" were separated, reason could on the one hand reinforce the *universalism* in practical validity claims, beyond the boundaries between the different religious communities,[78] but on the other, it would only be able to replace the lost ("de-sacralized") "binding force" through the "weak force of motivation" connected to good reasons.[79]

Habermas closes by emphasizing that he (in this work) has aimed to show how the transmission of "theological content"[80] into profane thinking may be framed as a *"philosophically recognisable learning process"*. To the extent that this has been a successful endeavour, he hopes that this may "encourage" the use of "our reasonable freedom".[81] At the same time, he expresses a hope that practice-based religious communities will be able to continue being a "thorn in the flesh"[82] of modern secular societies so that modern societies will remain open to "translations" of religious experiences and practices into the profane.

In this brief outline of Habermas' closing remarks in his postscript, I have stayed close to Habermas' own formulations. For, it is striking, when reading the final pages, how modestly and cautiously he expresses himself. This applies both to *what he himself may have accomplished* and his hopes for *the*

---

73 Habermas 2019, vol. II, p. 801, cf. point (iii) in the footnote above.
74 Habermas 2019, vol. II, pp. 784–785; *"aller* möglicherweise Betroffenen", p. 785.
75 Original: "Nachdem sich dann das Wissen vom Glauben getrennt hatte, …". Habermas 2019, vol. 2, p. 804.
76 Original: "Die säkulare Moderne hat sich aus guten Gründen vom Transzendenten abgewendet". Habermas, vol. II, p. 807, first sentence of the final paragraph on the final page.
77 In this and the following paragraph, I have purposely stayed close to Habermas' own formulations. Final sentence in the original: "aber die Vernunft würde mit dem Verschwinden jeden Gedankens, der das in der Welt Seiende im Ganzen transzendiert, selber verkümmern". Habermas 2019, vol. II, p. 807. Note that Habermas uses the subjunctive mood (*würde*); in other words: he expresses himself cautiously.
78 Habermas, vol. II, p. 804.
79 Habermas 2019, vol. II, p. 804.
80 "theologische[r] Gehalte", Habermas 2019, vol. 2, p. 806.
81 Habermas 2019, vol. 2, p. 806.
82 2 Corinthians 12:7

92 Religion in modern societies

role of religion in modern societies.[83] It is rather like a pious hope of "reasonable freedom", on the one hand, and of modern societies' willingness to open for "translation" of religious experiences on the other.

My comments

Here follow my comments on this grand and impressive scholarly *oeuvre*:

"Auch eine Geschichte der Philosophie" – linear and personal

There are many ways of writing a history of philosophy, different angles, and different selections.[84] Habermas has written a *remarkably linear* history of philosophy: the development moves steadily in one direction. And *remarkably personal*, in the sense that the Western history of philosophy is assessed on the basis of, and leads to, Habermas' own philosophy. Fair enough, but perhaps we should have been notified about this. Then again, perhaps the title provides a hint: "*Auch eine Geschichte der Philosophie*" ("*Also a History of Philosophy*"). Perhaps "*auch eine*" could be read as "*meine*": "*Auch eine* Geschichte der Philosophie" understood as "*Meine* Geschichte der Philosophie" ("*My* History of Philosophy")?

But regardless of the angle and philosophical orientation, it is a challenge that the *language* is often *less clear and precise* than it should have been. This applies, e.g., to the use of the word "religion" (as mentioned several times in this chapter). Here, a more precise use of concepts[85] would have been an advantage – both scholarly and philosophically – in order to *understand* what is said, but also concerning the *practical implications*.[86]

The diagnosis of our time – on point?

There is an array of challenges in modern societies. Habermas is well aware of this. At the same time, it is remarkable that he puts so much emphasis on

---

83 To invoke a Norwegian turn of phrase: He plays on a sordino, rather than on kettledrums and trombones.

84 Hence, Bertrand Russell wrote *A History of Western Philosophy*, 1945, assessing previous philosophers from the parameter of his own (analytical) philosophy.

85 Or "choice of words", as one and the same word may refer to different "concepts". We here note the useful exercise in interpretation and precision in Arne Næss' *ELE* (*En del elementære logiske emner*); English version: 1966: *Communication and Argument: Elements of Applied Semantics*. Translated by Alastair Hannay.

86 Here, we also touch upon the question as to how *universal and abstract*, or rather *detailed and specific*, the use of language ought to be, in different philosophical contexts. Cf., e.g., my comments, on this issue, in *Philosophie der Moderne*, Velbrück Wissenschaft, Weilerswist 2017, pp. 6–68. Here, in Habermas' work, his aim is not merely theoretical but also practical, considering how the world conditions change through time, and precisely for this reason, a universal and abstract use of concepts might be rather unfortunate.

90 Religion in modern societies

a focus on communicative and discursive reason and deliberative democracy in well-ordered states based on the rule of law.[67]

In his account of these thinkers (the "young Hegelians"), Habermas emphasizes the ambiguous in what he calls the "backdrop of life-worlds" or the "socialised and assimilated tradition".[68] Ambiguous, because such "backdrops" simultaneously *open up* and *close*; they are simultaneously "enabling and repressive".[69] They may *liberate* the individual, but they may also *delimit* individual autonomy. Therefore, we need critique through solid justification.[70]

Postscript: status, and hope

In the *postscript*, Habermas takes a twofold perspective (i) towards the "precarious status" of "reasonable freedom"[71] and (ii) towards the potentially positive role of religion in maintaining motivation and social unity.

After a retrospective summary, Habermas here makes a "shift of perspective", from "observer" to "participant",[72] and once again, religion is a core

---

67 The structure in Habermas' work from 2019, which reconstructs the history of philosophy as a development leading to Habermas' own position, is in many ways similar to the structure in the book *Paradigmen der Ersten Philosophie. Zur reflexiven – transzendentalpragmatischen – Rekonstruktion der Philosophiegeschichte* by Karl-Otto Apel, from 2011 (at the age of 89). Here, Apel operates with *three main paradigms* (p. 11): (i) *ontological metaphysics* (Greek philosophy and Medieval philosophy, which Apel characterises as "dogmatic"; "weil sie von einem quasigöttlichen Standpunkt externer Sicht der Welt als eines begrenzten Ganzen entworfen ist", p. 7 in Apel's book), (ii) *classic transcendental philosophy* (based on the "conscious subject" (*des Bewußtseinssubjekts*), and (iii) *the transcendental semiotic* based in a *community of communication and interpretation*, i.e., Apel's own philosophy. In Habermas' work from 2019, there is no reference to Apel's book.

68 Habermas 2019, vol. II, pp. 579–582.

69 Habermas 2019, vol. II, p. 581, "ermöglichend[en] und repressiv[en]".

70 But is this not the same issue that we previously referred to as *meaning-constitutive horizons* and which we connected to religion and to the role of religion as social-integrative force? But if so, why was the *ambiguity*, and therefore the *need for critique*, not more explicitly emphasized in the discussion of *religion* as horizon and as motivational force? It is rather conspicuous that Habermas does not elaborate on the internal theological discussion and critiques of religion. This applies to contributions such as Hans Jonas' *Der Gottesbegriff nach Auschwitz. Eine jüdische Stimme* (1984/1987) and *Der Platz zum Glauben* (2013), by the Kantian and theistic philosopher Peter Rohs, but also classical contributions, such as Leibniz on "the problem of evil" (published in 1710, prior to the earthquake and tsunami in Lisbon in 1755). None of these thinkers (or their writings) are mentioned in this comprehensive *oeuvre*.

71 Habermas 2019, vol. II, p. 778, see also pp. 778–807.

72 Original: "vom Beobachter zum Teilnehmer", Habermas 2019, vol. II, p. 777. In this postscript, Habermas operates with four points (vol. II, p. 778 fn.): (i) the importance of the participant-perspective, in *second-person* and in *first-person plural*; (ii) issues (and examples) of *moral progress*; (iii) the issue of "the motivational roots of moral learning-processes" [which is the basic theme with regard to religion as social-integrative force]; and (iv) the status of "reasonable freedom" in modern secular societies [which is the second basic theme: the need for communicative and discursive reason, in modern societies].

principles. Conversely, Habermas regards Kant as an advocate for universally valid reason and personal autonomy. Kant defends not only theoretical reason but also practical reason, and in his justification of universally valid normative principles (cf. the categorical imperative), Kant draws on the religious (Christian) legacy, understood as a precondition for his moral principles to make sense, in Kant's reasoning.[63]

History and man-made culture: language and "objective spirit"

But Kant remains within the subject-oriented paradigm, with the distinction between the thinking subject and the external world understood through the categories of the natural sciences (cf. Newton). Another shift emerges with the new cultural sciences, focusing on history and national languages: Herder and his fellow hermeneuticians focus on language as intersubjective and historically created horizons of understanding. And with Hegel, history becomes the central focus, as a dialectic *bildung* and learning process, where religion too, particularly Western Christianity, plays an important role.

Marx, Kierkegaard, Peirce, and pragmatism

In the perspective of *Hegel*, Kant's transcendental-philosophical point is "*situated*" in the historical *bildung* process. Thereafter follows what Habermas refers to as a "de-transcendentalization",[64] focusing on the lifeforms of bodily and socially communicative persons: In *Marx'* perspective, Hegelian points become "situated" with a focus on socio-economic factors and class.[65] In *Kierkegaard's* perspective, Hegelian points become "situated" and transformed in an existential language, with a focus on "*hin Enkelte*" (the single individual) and on different "stages" in the life cycle.[66] And with *Peirce* and the *North American pragmatism*, the thinking process is "situated" in different kinds of practices, which are also open for normative learning, with a focus on language and communication and on academic communities as a basis for reasonable seeking of truth. The culmination of this trend means situating communicative and discursive use of reason in the academic community and in politics – in other words, in *Habermas' own philosophy*, with

---

63 Then again, one might say that Kant does not contribute much with regard to "strong moral motivation", while Hume may have more to say about motivation based on his empiricism, cf. *A Treatise of Human Nature, Book II*, from 1739 (mentioned in Habermas 2019, vol. 2, p. 228 fn.). Hence, we might conclude that Kant is strong when it comes to justification but not on the issue of motivation; for Hume, it is to a certain extent the other way around.
64 In those he considers "young-Hegelians" (including Peirce).
65 Where socio-economic factors, the "base", have a decisive impact on ideas and forms of consciousness in the "superstructure".
66 From everyday life to the aesthetic, through to the ethical, and finally, to the religious stage.

social integration, and hence on "religion" as a response to these challenges, with a particular focus on the development of the interplay between Western Christianity and philosophy. But is this on point, considering all of the other challenges we are faced with today?

The climate crisis, for instance, does not hold a central place in Habermas. True enough, he mentions "climate change" (climate change, not climate crisis), e.g., in the postscript. But he immediately adds that the "physical predictions" are relatively indisputable and that the effects are so unavoidable that the international community might be able to meet these challenges, in due time, through the classic measures of international law.[87]

A remarkably optimistic take, considering the challenges we and future generations are faced with – challenges which may develop to become quite dramatic, at the same time as our institutions, including democratic and legal institutions, may have trouble handling these challenges in due time[88]:

An *election-based democracy* may easily be too short-sighted. Winning the next election becomes more important than addressing these long-term challenges. Employment and salaries in the present easily gain privilege above vital needs for future generations.

Sure enough, with *legislative measures* we might "tie ourselves to the mast". But current legislation is a matter of political decision. Which brings us back where we started, in politics. At the same time, political decisions are affected by the forming of opinion in the public sphere, and by different forms of professional knowledge, and by the quality of the critique of science.[89] In short, this calls for self-critical treatment of the various sciences, as a practice and a learning process.[90]

---

87 Habermas 2019, vol. II, p. 799, has relatively little to say about ecological challenges: "Aber ökologische Risiken sind auf der Grundlage physikalischer Voraussagen relativ unstrittig und in ihren imminenten Auswirkungen unausweichlich. Daher könnte es noch rechtzeitig gelingen, dass die internationale Gemeinschaft dieser globalen Herausforderungen sogar mit den klassischen Instrumenten des Völkerrechts begegnet". This is all he is prepared to say on this matter. However, he uses the subjunctive mode (*könnte*); thus, he expresses himself cautiously and modestly. In the subsequent sentence, he shifts the focus to the challenges concerning power relations in internet communication and to the "dramatic consequences of an unlimited manipulation of the human genome" (a topic that has occupied him for a long time, cf. the book *Die Zukunft der menschlichen Natur. Auf dem Weg zu einer liberalen Eugenik?* from 2001 /English translation *The Future of Human Nature* Polity Press, Cambridge 2003), and here Habermas uses the word "dramatic" – a word he does not invoke when addressing "climate change". (Nor does he mention biotechnological measures for general *human enhancement*, cf. *transhumanism* and *singularity*, according to Raymond Kurzweil, mentioned in Skirbekk, *Philosophie der Moderne*, 2017, pp. 59–63.)
88 A reference to what I have in mind here, cf. the discussion of crises in Skirbekk, *Epistemic Challenges in a Moderne World*, 2019.
89 And different kinds of power relations.
90 "Philosophy of science" as elaborated upon above, in the initial text: "Science and Religion".

94 Religion in modern societies

Here, there are two levels of knowledge-related challenges. On the one hand, professional knowledge, in our time, tends to become more and more specialized, and narrow – while the problems become more complex and require an interplay of several perspectives. On the other hand, crises and complexity may make vulnerable groups feel a need for simple and strong "answers" – a trend which may become reinforced by one-sided and emotional statements in social media – while the situation at hand would ideally require enlightened citizens rather than people who believe in *fake news* and creative conspiracy theories.

In other words, in addition to the challenges "in the world", modern societies in crisis are facing knowledge-related challenges. Strong motivation is not enough. Strong motivation without sufficient enlightenment may be a slippery slope. In addition to motivation, enlightenment and general education are important factors. This includes informed critique of science and a certain degree of competence in the philosophy of science.

In short, some of our current *climate-related, institution-related*, and *knowledge-related challenges* are not granted much attention in Habermas' work from 2019. In this sense, the diagnosis of our time is not entirely on point.

Religion as a response – on point, then and now?

If the challenge is impediments to social integration and the answer is religion, then *what is the evidence?* The proposition that rites and myths were important to ensure solidarity and unity in early tribal societies is thoroughly discussed by Habermas, with extensive references to central thinkers and writings from the sociological classic by Émile Durkheim (1858–1917) to sociologists of religion such as Robert Bellah (1927–2013).[91]

This is not my field, but as far as I can tell, Habermas has reasonably strong support, for his perspectives, in the academic literature he goes through. But even if it is true that "religion", in the form of rites and myths, was important for unity and solidarity in societies *in earlier times*, it is not given that this is the case today, in complex and globalized societies. Hence, the question: What is the evidence that "religion" is important for unity and solidarity *in our time as well?*[92]

---

91 Cf., e.g., Durkheim, *Les formes élémentaires de la vie religieuse* ("The Elementary Forms of the Religious Life") from 1912, and Bellah, *Religion in Human Evolution. From the Paleolithic to the Axial Age*, from 2011.

92 Again, Durkheim is a classic, with his sociological work on suicide, *Le suicide* from 1897 (*Suicide*, first translated to English in 1951), where Durkheim considers suicide an expression of a lack of unity. Here, he takes a statistical approach to mapping the extent of suicide based on different categories, such as married vs. unmarried, Catholic vs. Protestant, in addition to factors such as sex, age, and class. And yes, in this material, religion (particularly Catholicism) has a *positive* effect: fewer suicides, more unity.

This question cannot be answered by way of a historical outline alone. In order to find out whether (or how) "religion" in any significant way contributes to unity in modern globalized societies, extensive research and interpretation are required, where one *distinguishes between* "religion" and "religion" (i.e. the language must be precise), and where one approaches the different aspects of this problem complex *in our current societies*. A historical outline of previous debates and trends is not enough.

Neither does it help to appeal to the thesis that we live in a *post-secular* society, where "religion" (despite prediction from secular theory) plays an important part. For the question is what this means, in different contexts, and again, what is needed is conceptual clarification and nuanced research and interpretation, in order to find out.

In addition, the question emerges of whether *all* "religions" contribute to more unity and solidarity in our world today, or whether, in some cases, it might be the other way around – namely, that "religion" also may create division and struggle, internally and externally. For instance, what about the relationship between religion and politics in countries like Iran, Saudi Arabia, and Turkey in this sense?[93] And what about the role of religion in non-state armed groups that repeatedly create war-like situations?[94] And what about religious indoctrination of children and adolescents, with the risk of impeded personal autonomy in adulthood?[95] In short, premodern and politicized versions of "religion" do not always promote unity and solidarity – not globally and universally, for all who live today, and neither with regard to future generations.

In other words, if "social integration" is the current problem (but there are several other problems in the world today, which are often intertwined and mutually reinforcing), then "religion" is not *the only* remedy; other aspects may impact this, such as marital status and family relations. Neither is it reasonable to think that *all kinds* of religion and religious practice will have a social-integrative function; e.g., contemplation and theoretical studies of theology are not likely to have such an impact, at least not immediately.

---

93 Cf. "religion" as "social integration" in the face of a military-religious superpower in the following chapter on Ahmet Kuru.

94 Cf. Herfried Münkler, *Die neuen Kriege* [The New Wars]; Rowolt Verlag, Hamburg 2002; and Hans Jakob Orning and Øyvind Østerud, *Krig uten stat* [War without State], Dreyers Forlag, Oslo 2020.

95 Cf. Habermas' note of the risk that appropriated traditions may be repressive and damaging for personal autonomy (vol. II, pp. 580–581). Again, we recall Ludvig Holberg, on the same risk: "Children must be made into human beings before they become Christians; ... But we begin by the catechization of divine secrets, and as a result everyone defends with extreme obstinacy the sect in which he has been brought up and is not receptive to any arguments [...]". *Moral reflections and epistles*, ed. P.M. Mitchell, 1991, pp. 13–14; and furthermore: "If one learns theology before one learns to become a human being, one will never become a human being". *Moral Reflections and Epistles*, ed. P.M Mitchell, 1991, p. 15. (What would Holberg say about Qur'an schools?)

96 Religion in modern societies

Moreover, there are religious variants that may, quite the contrary, be *counterproductive* with regard to successful social integration from a global perspective – religious groups that exercise exclusive group-internal identity and solidarity, and that may easily create division and struggle rather than unity and solidarity in a universal perspective.

In short, referring to *unspecified* "religion" as the major remedy against declining social integration in today's complicated and globalized society is hardly on point.[96]

The need for conceptual precision

In other words, in this *oeuvre*, there is a need for more precision with regard to central words, such as "religion", or "translation",[97] or "solidarity".[98] For, it makes a difference, in practical terms as well, whether we mean one thing or the other when we talk about "religion", or "translation", or "solidarity".

The thesis (or hypothesis) that "religion" may be important for successful social integration, in our time as well, could have appeared as more credible and could have been more convincingly supported, if the language had been more precise, such that it was clear and unequivocal what is meant by "religion" in this context.

If so, it would be possible to distinguish between that and the other, i.e. between religions (or religious variants) that have gone through some "modernization of consciousness", and those that have not. Then, it would be possible to form a well-founded opinion on what it might be, in religion, in different forms, that potentially constitute a foundation for certain forms of unity and solidarity in today's globalized world.

---

96 True enough, it is possible to read Habermas in the sense that he, with "religion" (in modern societies) means "Western Christianity", more specifically: Western Christianity that has gone through an internal modernization (cf. Habermas' thesis of the "modernization of consciousness" e.g. Habermas 2005, p. 146/ English translation *Between Naturalism and Religion*, Wiley, 2014, p. 136). But if so, this should be stated explicitly. And if so, the case should be convincingly argued that the learning processes and translations connected to "Western Christianity" are relevant for all, including, e.g., China and the Muslim world. Moreover, what is "Western"? Through immigration, Europe is impacted by other religions than (Western) Christianity. And at that, the United States (which Habermas refers to as a "spearhead of modernisation", cf. Habermas 2019, vol. I, p. 81) suffers in many ways from a lack of enlightened critique of religion, cf., e.g., the "evangelicals", who, based on an uncritical and literal reading of the Bible (including the Old Testament), contribute to exerting an unfortunate influence on American politics, *inter alia* in the Middle East.

97 "Translate" what and how? Translate statements, or concepts, or "world-pictures", or "tacit knowledge" (connected to rites or other forms of practice)?

98 "Solidarity", towards whom? Towards everyone, or towards the weak and those in need, or towards our own people (in some way or another), as opposed to the others? Solidarity towards those who live today, or towards future generations as well?

7

ISLAM IN A HISTORICAL CLASS PERSPECTIVE

Ahmet T. Kuru

Personal background

In 2019, as a professor in political science at the San Diego State University, Ahmet T. Kuru (b. 1972), published the book *Islam, Authoritarianism, and Underdevelopment: A Global and Historical Comparison.*[1] In the preface, he starts by referring to the background: He grew up in a Muslim family in Turkey. One day, at breakfast, in 1989, his father was upset. The previous day, the family had had a dinner visit from a secular Turkish general. Around midnight, the discussion became heated. The general had claimed that the Muslim world was "backward" and that it is the West, particularly Protestant nations, that truly contributed to modern civilization. His father was frustrated. And the young Ahmet was presented with a question that he has pondered ever since: Is it true that the Muslim world is backward compared to the West? And if so, why? Ahmet Kuru becomes a social scientist, ends up in the United States, and writes the book *Islam, Authoritarianism, and Underdevelopment*, dedicated to his father, *post-mortem*, and his two Turkish-American sons.

---

1 Cambridge University Press, New York, 2019. A book of 303 pages; 237 pages of text, 11 pages of index, and a bibliography of 55 pages (Kuru is no lightweight!). Quote from the website of San Diego State University, referring to Ahmet Kuru's book: "*Islam, Authoritarianism, and Underdevelopment: A Global and Historical Comparison* (Cambridge University Press, 2019) became the co-winner of the American Political Science Association's International History and Politics Section Book Award. Kuru's works have been translated into Arabic, Bosnian, Chinese, French, Indonesian, and Turkish."

DOI: 10.4324/9781003441618-11

98 Religion in modern societies

The current situation

So, what is the current situation in countries with a Muslim majority? (Who was right – the general or the father?) Ahmet Kuru raises the question on the first page of the book. On the next page, he presents the following numbers (from ca. 2010) for 49 countries with a Muslim majority on the one hand, and for "all countries" (ca. 195), on the other: (1) electoral democracies, 14% *vs.* 60%; (2) averages of gross national income per capita (*GNIpc*), \$9,000 *vs.* \$ 14.000; (3) literacy rate, 73% *vs.* 84%; (4) years of schooling 5.8 years *vs.* 7.5; (5) life expectancy, 60 years *vs.* 69.[2] The numbers tell us that the current situation for the countries with a Muslim majority is not very good. But in earlier days, from the eighth to the twelfth century, it was quite a different matter.

How could this be? Why are countries with a Muslim majority today less democratic and less developed than most other countries?[3] And why was this quite different in earlier days, from the eighth century through to the twelfth century? These are the basic questions of the book *Islam, Authoritarianism, and Underdevelopment.*

Two well-known perceptions that cannot be true

Kuru refers to two well-known and contradictory views. (i) One claims that Islam and cultural progress are simply incompatible entities. This view, he refers to as *essentialism.* (ii) The other claims that the decline is a result of Western colonialism and repression. This view, he refers to as *post-colonialism.* The first view blames Islam as a religion. The second view blames the West and acquits the Muslim world.

Based on a historical account, from the eighth to the eighteenth century, Kuru rejects both of these perceptions – in short:

> In the period from the eighth century and well into the eleventh century, Muslim countries were doing well. Economically and culturally, the Muslim world was prominent. Islam and progress went hand in hand. Hence, Islam (*per se*) cannot be the problem. In this sense, the "essentialists" are wrong.
>
> At the same time, the historical account shows that the decline in the Muslim world started at the end of the Medieval Age, i.e. before the Western states inserted themselves. Hence, Western colonialism and repression cannot explain the stagnation of the Muslim world. In this sense, the "post-colonialists" are wrong.

---

2 Reference: Freedom House 2013, The World Bank 2010, UN Statistics Division 2013, and for the two last ones: The UN's Development Programme 2011.

3 Direct quote, p. 1: "Why are Muslim-majority countries less peaceful, less democratic, less developed?" It is worth noting here that Kuru is a Muslim. He cannot be rejected as an "Islamophobe".

Explanation: Four classes and changes in the relationship between classes over time

What, then, might explain the decline of the Muslim world? Kuru points to *class*, to the shifts in the relationship between the classes. This is what he does in the book, in a historical account of the *shifts* in *class constellations* in the Muslim world, in a comparative perspective, where he categorizes *four classes*: (i) those with military and political power, (ii) religious leaders, (iii) merchants, and (iv) scholars.

The basic framework of Kuru's historically based argumentation is this: As long as the four classes operated relatively freely and independently from each other, the Muslim world was prosperous. Kuru refers to the period from the eighth century to the eleventh century. In this period, the Muslim world was successful, in many ways more so than the contemporary Western states, not only in terms of military and administration but also economically, scientifically, and intellectually. But with time, changes occurred in the class constellations. Military and political leaders and the religious elites united in a concentration of power at the top of society; religious leaders provided legitimacy for the politico-military actors, who in turn provided support for religious leaders.[4] At this point, the Muslim world started its decline.

This contrasts with the development in the Western world. There we have, according to Kuru, in many ways the opposite trajectory[5]: In the early Medieval Age, after the fall of Rome, Western societies were weak. But then, as the eleventh century progresses, a separation between Church and State, between pope and king, occurs in several states. And free city-states are formed, in Northern Italy and in North-Western Europe, with a relatively strong and independent upper class of merchants. At the same time, relatively independent universities[6] are established, with different disciplines[7] – a meeting place for teachers and students, with a fair degree of academic freedom. Then follows the Renaissance, the Reformation, the new experimental and mathematically formulated natural sciences, and the Enlightenment Age – in the Western world.

In short, what happens in the West is virtually the opposite of what happens in the Muslim world – seen from Kuru's framework of the four classes:

---

4 This is a kind of religious and politico-military power concentration that we recognize in today's world as well: the "theocracy" in Iran, the family dynasty in Saudi Arabia, and Turkey under Erdogan – historically, these were the three rivalling power centres: respectively, the Persian, the Arab, and the Ottoman.

5 Kuru is sceptical towards forced top-down secularization by authoritarian regimes; in this regard, he refers to Atatürk and Nasser.

6 Such as in Bologna, Salerno, Montpellier, Paris, and Oxford.

7 Such as law, theology, medicine, and philosophy, in addition to basic training in disciplines in the natural sciences and in the 'liberal arts' (*quadrivium*: geometry, arithmetic, astronomy, and music, and *trivium*: grammar, rhetoric, dialectic). Cf. Skirbekk/Gilje. *A History of Western Thought: From Ancient Greece to the Twentieth Century*. Routledge, London 2001, pp. 142–145.

100 Religion in modern societies

At the time when military and religious leaders in the Muslim world unite in one dominating alliance of power, at the expense of both the merchant class and the scholars, the opposite occurs in the Western world, where the four classes in different ways become more independent. This leads to a decline in the Muslim world and to prosperity in the West. The roles are reversed in accordance with changes in the relationship between the classes.

The framework is simple. But the argumentation is clear and consistent.[8] In so far, the book is a "must" for those interested in this issue. Before I proceed to my comments, I will provide a few brief glimpses of some of the topics that Kuru discusses, in addition to, but in expansion of, what he says about class relations.

Printing presses and popular enlightenment

It is often the case that the classes that hold a lot of power are not very "pro-change", especially the kind of change and innovation that may challenge their own power position. In these cases, religious leaders may be a convenient asset, if they may contribute to keeping people loyal and obedient, e.g. through mutual rites and myths that provide identification with the rulers and the state-endorsing religion.

On the other hand, popular enlightenment, along with free and open discussion, may impede obedience towards those holding power, both political and religious. In this regard, technology is also important: With Johann Gutenberg (ca. 1400–1468) and the art of printing, books and pamphlets were soon mass-produced, in Western Europe. The Bible was printed in 1455. According to Kuru, there were, in 1480, book printers in more than 100 Western-European cities.[9]

The Reformation and the Bible printed in the mother's tongue (through Luther's German translation in the mid-sixteenth century) made for a boost in general reading and popular enlightenment. According to Kuru, three million books were printed in Europe in 1550, more than the number of manuscripts published in the entire fourteenth century.[10]

The contrast to the situation in the Muslim world in this period is striking: Not a single book was printed in a state under Muslim rule until the year 1729 (in the Ottoman Empire). That is 274 years after the first printing of the Bible.

Moreover, the religious leaders in the Ottoman Empire (*ulema*) were strongly opposed to the translation of the Qur'an to Turkish, the mother tongue of large parts of the population of this empire. Only in 1924 (after the establishment of the Turkish Republic) did the first complete edition of the

---

8 Kuru refers to the scholarly literature with an ample bibliography of 55 pages.
9 Kuru 2019, p. 187.
10 According to Kuru's references pp. 187–188.

Qur'an in Turkish become published.[11] Ahmet Kuru estimates that literacy in the Ottoman Empire around the year 1800 was about 1%, whereas in Europe, it was more than 30% in the same period.[12]

State remuneration and stagnation

At times, higher officials, particularly in the military, were remunerated through land allotted by the state, not as private property nor as property to be inherited by future generations,[13] but as a right of use for each individual state official – the so-called iqta system.[14]

Based on this system, there were few incentives for long-term investments in the property one had at one's disposal, as there would be with private ownership, where the land may be sold or inherited.[15] Hence, it made sense to engage in short-term exploitation of the land and its inhabitants.

With this form of remuneration, state officials were economically dependent on the state rulers. And as the land had often been confiscated or occupied, state officials, as a group, had a vested interest in the state expanding and conquering new land. In short, this system ensured loyalty towards the ruling class, while also contributing to the militarization of the state. And, we could add: Based on this system (*iqta*), it was difficult for ambitious actors to build up their own economic political power base that would be a viable rival for the central power.[16]

At the same time, Kuru emphasizes that this system contributed to impeding the market forces, and hence the class of merchants. And this, in turn, led to the scholars becoming more dependent on financial support from the state power elite, which, with time, restrained innovation and creativity.[17]

---

11 Kuru 2019, pp. 207–212, "Printing Presses and Quran Translations". Quote, p. 211: "Because of the ulema's opposition, the printing of the first complete Turkish translation of the Quran became possible only in 1924, a year after the foundation of the Turkish Republic". On the same general issue, cf. also Mohammed Ghaly, "The Interplay of Technology and Sacredness in Islam: Discussions of Muslim Scholars on Printing the Qur'an", *Studies in Ethics, Law, and Technology*, 3(2), Article 3: 2009, pp. 1-24.

12 Kuru 2019, p. 207. In the Danico-Norwegian state, the confirmation preparation (which involved reading of Holy Scriptures) was obligatory for all, boys and girls, from around the 1730s. In the early nineteenth century, in Norway, literacy was quite extensive. Cf. Jostein Fet, *Lesande bønder* [*Reading Farmers*], Oslo 1995, Lis Flyberg, «I bondens hyller: en 1700-talls bonde og hans bøker» [*In the Bookshelf of a 18th Century Farmer and His Books*], *Heimen*, 48: 2011, pp. 31–46.

13 Kuru 2019, p. 99.

14 Kuru 2019, pp. 98–101.

15 Kuru 2019, pp. 98–101.

16 Cf. the Western European nobility, in the tension between fiefdom (borrowed land) and private property, but at times as relatively independent political actors, based on their own powerbase.

17 Kuru 2019, p. 107.

102 Religion in modern societies

Philosophical anti-philosophy and support for the alliance between state and ulema

In addition to these trends posed by the economic organization, the late eleventh century saw central spokespersons, such as al-Ghazali (1058–1111), actively and effectively supporting the alliance between state and *ulema* (religious leaders),[18] who also initiated a campaign against freethinking philosophers,[19] advocating the protection of Islam against Greek thinking and "foreign" (non-Islam) sciences.[20]

Kuru emphasizes that also the importance of this internal battle among the "scholars" must be acknowledged, in this regard: it led to ostracization and marginalization of critical thinking in the Muslim world.[21]

Main accusation: not Islam, not the West, but shifts in the class relations

The main point, for Kuru, is that it was not Islam *per se* that caused the decline of the Muslim world. The decline was primarily a result of the shifts in the class relations, first and foremost through the merging of the two classes on top, the military and religious leaders, and, as a corollary, a deterioration of the previously more independent merchants and the previously more independent scholars.

At the outset of this decline, around year 1100, it was primarily due to these shifts in class relations. This was the main reason; this is where to place the blame! Not in Islam, as a religion, for it had been there all along, from the eighth century and onwards, when the Muslim world prospered energetically, scientifically as well as culturally.[22] But neither is the blame to be placed

---

18 Kuru 2019, p. 110. Cf. the quote from Ghazali about the relationship of mutual interests between state and religion (Kuru 2019, p. 112 footnote 269): "[T]he state and religion are twins. Religion is the foundation while the state is the guard. That which has no foundation will certainly crumble and that which has no guard is lost".

19 Quote, Kuru 2019, p. 110: "By declaring philosophers with certain views apostates to be killed, Ghazali made the 'orthodox views' almost unquestionable".

20 Kuru 2019, pp. 103–104. Cf. also Skirbekk/Gilje. *A History of Western Thought: From Ancient Greece to the Twentieth Century*. Routledge, London 2001, pp. 145–148.

21 Kuru 2019, p. 112: "Later on, critical thinking on religious and metaphysical issues was so discouraged that Islamic civilization rarely produced Islamic scholars and philosophers of the calibre of Ghazali [!] and Ibn Sina again" (my brackets).

22 We might also ask whether this connection was present in the time of Muhammed as well, as he was a military as well as a religious leader. Kuru raises the question on page 94 but abandons the point by referring to Muhammed's leadership as a personal and charismatic one, rather than a class- or state-based one. This might well be, but the question remains whether this military-religious double role in Muhammed may have made it easier to promote and accept a "collaboration of the classes" between military and religious leaders at a later stage in history.

on the Western world, because the decline in the Muslim world began *before* the Western world inserted itself and was primarily caused by internal class relations.[23]

Comments

The basic thesis, and the historical account, are clear and potent, not to mention rich in implications. But the book nevertheless opens for different kinds of comments. I will here limit myself to one general point: The book is motivated by a concern for *the current situation* in the Muslim world. But the theme of the book is the *historical background*: the period from the eighth century into recent times, outlined with an escalating pace towards the twentieth century when the Ottoman Empire fell. And at the end, a brief conclusion,[24] where Ahmet Kuru delivers the following bold statement: "No Intelligentsia/Bourgeoisie, No Development".[25] The final paragraph states the following:

> In order to solve the problems of violence, authoritarianism, and underdevelopment, as well as catch up to Western levels of development, Muslims should establish competitive and meritocratic systems. These will require substantial socioeconomic and political reform with ideological and institutional dimensions. For such a reform to take place, Muslims need creative intellectuals and an independent bourgeoisie, who can balance the power of the ulema and state authorities.[26]

In other words, Kuru makes relatively few statements about *modern societies* and *the situation in the world today.* Nor does he claim to do so. But at the same time, it was current problems that motivated him to write the book and which he returns to in the final paragraph, where he delivers the previously cited appeal. In this sense, there is a certain discrepancy between the underlying problem complex, which motivated him, and the topic of the book, as primarily a historical account.

Of course, the historical account is not irrelevant for the current situation, in the Muslim world or elsewhere. In no way. Such an account is undoubtedly important, particularly with regard to the Muslim world, where the reference to and interpretation of history often plays an important part in our understanding of the current situation as well.

---

23 In addition, Kuru discusses the thesis that the reinforcement of the military towards the end of the Medieval Age might be connected to the Mongolian invasion from the East and the crusades from the West, contributing to creating an impression of the armed forces as particularly important. Kuru 2019, pp. 119–122.
24 Kuru 2019, pp. 227–235.
25 Kuru 2019, p. 232
26 Kuru 2019, p. 235.

104 Religion in modern societies

Then again, this means that several of the specific challenges, which affect us all, in modern societies, are not addressed in this book. We here recall what we have said earlier in this publication about challenges and crises in modern science-based and institutionally differentiated societies.

Comments – Kuru versus Habermas

Social integration, with religion as a central precondition, is fundamental in Habermas. The terms are not crystal clear. But Habermas makes it clear that he is primarily talking about Western Christianity.

He does not address Islam, although today Islam is an important religion within as well as outside of Europe.[27] Here Kuru represents an important corrective, first, by addressing Islam, and second, by noting that "religion" in the hands of *ulema*, and in alliance with the state rulers, may have a repressive impact on social integration, in quite a different way than what Habermas would like when he speaks warmly of "social integration".

The point is not that Habermas is blind to such circumstances, nor that he would deny that this may be the case in given places. But it demonstrates, once again, how important it is that we adequately specify and contextualize central words and concepts, such as "religion" and "social integration". And by extension, how important it is that we include unfortunate forms of social integration and the kind of "identity-founding" motivation which in different instances are produced by various forms of social control and ritual-based indoctrination.

Kuru's book is thus an important corrective to Habermas' work by reminding us of "what is missing", both with regard to conceptual precision and with regard to the theme. Islam, which Kuru addresses, is today one of the religions in the "European West". Therefore, it is recommendable to read Kuru's book in parallel with Habermas' work, where Islam is conspicuously absent and where problematic aspects of certain forms of religiously motivated "social integration" are not adequately communicated.

Comments – the Norwegian context, by comparison

a) *Reading and popular enlightenment*
As Kuru has demonstrated: The Muslim world was originally an advanced civilization, from the eighth century and onwards. But as mentioned, the

---

27 "Here in the European West" ("Hier, im europäischen Westen"), as Habermas writes, in "Die Grenze zwischen Glauben und Wissen. Zur Wirkungsgeschichte und aktuellen Bedeutung von Kants Religionsphilosophie», *Revue de métaphysique et de morale*, nr. 44, 4/2004, pp. 460–484, fourth paragraph.

Islam in a historical class perspective **105**

development in book printing and general literacy was a slow one. In the Danico-Norwegian monarchy, confirmation was obligatory from the 1730s, for all adolescents, boys and girls, where readings of the Bible and the catechism were a central feature. And from the late nineteenth century and into the twentieth century, a common public school, for all, was established.[28]

b) *Classes*

Kuru operates with four classes, as we have seen, and sees the problem of the close alliance between military (political) and religious leaders. In Norway, after 1814, there were, roughly speaking, four classes (as nobility was abolished in 1821): state officials (lawyers and Lutheran theologians, in addition to military officers), the bourgeois (cf. the main characters of Ibsen's plays!), farmers (with private property or different kinds of tenant arrangements), and crofters and workers (of different kinds). Lawyers and theologians received their education at a state university. There they were socialized into a scientific culture, with colleagues in a pluralism of disciplines. This also applied to the theologians. And they gained their subsequent position based on their exams at the university, not inheritance or money. Through their education and position, they held a great influence, but their salaries were moderate. They were meritocrats in the sense that Francis Fukuyama advocates.[29]

c) *Popular movements, self-organization, and new institutions*

The transition *from tribal society to state* and the role of *religion* are important points, which have been extensively discussed. In this regard, it has been observed that when the Western Church, during the Medieval Age, gradually implemented restrictions to the marriage laws, with prohibitions against marriage between relatives (up to fifth cousin!),[30] the result was a broader interaction with people outside of the extended family and a weakening of the tribal system, and at the same time, it stimulated the transition to autonomous self-organization, such as craft unions in the new city-states.

In Norway, a range of *popular movements* emerged from the early nineteenth century, based on self-organization, from the religiously motivated lay movement built on Hans Nielsen Hauge's preaching and

---

28 Cf. e.g. Sverre Bagge, *Da boken kom til Norge; 1000–1537* [*When the book came to Norway*], Aschehoug, Oslo 2001.

29 Cf. Fukuyama's pointed appeal: "Getting to Denmark!", in Francis Fukuyama, *Political Order and Political Decay*, Farrar, Straus and Giroux, New York 2014.

30 Cf. Joseph Henrich, *The Weirdest People in the World. How the West Became Psychologically Peculiar and Particularly Prosperous*, Allen Lane Penguin Books, London 2020. Cf., e.g., the timetable (Table 5.2), pp. 168–169. Joseph Henrich is a professor of evolutionary biology at Harvard University.

106 Religion in modern societies

onwards.[31] Then there was the emergence of the contentious interplay between *Lutheran state officials* and *well-organized popular movements*, in a mutual learning process in different public fora, from the *Storting* (Parliament) and the municipal councils to pamphlets and newspapers,[32] a development that lasted until 1884, with the introduction of parliamentarianism and the subsequent establishment of political parties and trade unions.[33]

When the call for an election on the union between Norway and Sweden was announced in 1905, and only men had suffrage, women swiftly organized their own election and received a number of votes that corresponded to two-thirds of the male votes. In short, a great ability and willingness to self-organize!

And further, as the twentieth century progressed, laws were implemented for work life and family life,[34] a common public school for all, a fairly egalitarian political culture, with a relatively high degree of trust, in individuals and in institutions – all of this constitutes the backdrop for a universal and generous welfare state, which after the war gradually began to have some money to distribute, from national insurance to student loans. Quite unique and not always readily comprehended when seen from the outside.

d) *Kinds of knowledge and experiences*

As mentioned, the state officials – theologians and lawyers – received their education at the universities, from the early nineteenth century, at the university in Christiania. The theologians had to learn Latin, Greek, and Hebrew. That is not congenital, nor hereditary. In order to become a Lutheran priest, or a lawyer, one had to pass the exam at the university, a "*embetseksamen*" (a 'state official exam'). They were meritocrats.

The community was small. It is reasonable to assume that the professors knew each other, or at least knew of each other, across disciplines

---

31 Cf. Nils Gilje and Tarald Rasmussen, *Tankeliv i den lutherske stat; 1537–1814* (Aschehoug, Oslo 2002), which, *inter alia* refers to (p. 430) Hans Nielsen Hauge's authorship of 33 texts and 7 publications by other authors, with an estimated scope of 250,000 editions, during a period when the Norwegian population counted approximately 1 million (and with, at times, great poverty and destitution, cf. Ibsen's poem *Terje Vigen*; translated to English by Fydell Edmund Garrett and Axel Gerhard Dehly).

32 Such as *Statsborgeren* [*The Citizen*] published by Peder Soelvold (in the years 1831–1835; subsequently, for a short period, published by Henrik Wergeland). Cf., e.g., Marthe Hommerstad, *Politiske Bønder. Bondestrategene og kampen for demokratiet 1814–1837* [*Political farmers. The farmer strategists and the struggle for democracy 1814–1837*], Spartacus forlag, Oslo 2014. Cf. also Anders Johansen, *Å komme til orde. Politisk kommunikasjon 1814–1913* [*To get the word. Political communication 1814–1913*], Universitetsforlaget, Oslo 2019.

33 Cf. Gunnar Skirbekk, *Multiple Modernities. A Tale of Scandinavian Experiences*, The Chinese University Press, Hong Kong 2011, and "Processes of Modernisation. Scandinavian Experiences", *Transcultural Studies*, 2018.

34 With Johan Castberg as a prominent figure.

Islam in a historical class perspective **107**

and faculties, and that the same to some extent applied to the students. At least in the sense that they understood that they needed to watch their tongues lest they said something stupid that those in other disciplines would laugh at. It was not the same as receiving one's education at a private priest academy, in downtown Kansas City or another city in the Midwest, where Genesis was read in literal terms and where one was at liberty to disregard Darwin and Freud and the like. And the university-educated Norwegian theologians and lawyers knew that there are academic discussions, such as the doctoral defence, where candidates must face counterarguments.

Something similar applied to the followers of Hans Nielsen Hauge: They read and interpreted the Holy Scriptures, as good Lutherans and members of the State Church, but sometimes their perceptions differed from those of the priesthood. Likewise, they read and interpreted secular writings, e.g. legal documents, in situations where they were at variance with the legal frameworks and the state-employed lawyers – such as the outlook on gathering "friends" for private devotions.[35] Thus, they also gained experience and training in reasonable argumentation. They were trained in interpreting texts and putting forth arguments in public spaces – in short, in interpretative as well as argumentative reasoning. Moreover, they were skilled in practical matters, e.g. trade, crafts, and shipping. In short, in instrumental reasoning – in practical settings. On top of this, they learned to organize themselves and to speak up in public congregations.[36] In short, a practice-based competence.

The contentious interplay between state officials and popular movements carried with it learning processes along several dimensions. Useful for modern societies, useful for becoming decent persons and co-responsible citizens in a changing society. The material circumstances were often base in several ways. But for the educated class as well as for the population at large, the aspect of literacy and popular enlightenment was probably different in Lutheran Norway compared to Ottoman Turkey, and probably in Kemal Atatürk's republic as well.

---

35 Cf. the Conventicle Act (*Konventikkelplakaten*) of 1741 which prohibited religious meetings not authorized by the state church.
36 Cf. Anders Johansen, *Å komme til orde. Politisk kommunikasjon 1814–1913 [To get the word. Political communication 1814–1913]*, Universitetsforlaget, Oslo 2019.

8

RELIGION IN SCIENCE-BASED AND INSTITUTIONALLY DIFFERENTIATED SOCIETIES IN CRISIS

Concluding remarks

The unifying topic of this book is *religion in modern societies* – that is, *in science-based and institutionally differentiated societies in crisis* – and the overarching question, put bluntly, could be formulated thus: Is religion in modern societies a *problem or a resource*? Or both, *problem and resource*?

For, as we have seen, this is ambiguous. Partly because the topic is complex and multifaceted, partly because one may take different angles and approaches to the topic, and because we are, then, dealing with different concepts, and not rarely with an unclear and ambiguous use of concepts. Precisely for this reason, it might be useful to conduct the kind of outline that we have attempted throughout this book.

But, as we have seen, we are faced with the ambiguous use of concepts already at the outset, in the word "religion", with a subsequent need to clarify and contextualize. The same applies to the question of whether "religion" can be said to be unifying or divisive, whether religiously founded "social integration" mainly fosters universal solidarity[1] or conflict between cultures.[2]

To the extent that religion, in different forms, poses *problems* in modern societies – as worldview and life perception, or as a form of life and a pattern of action – *what should then be done*? I will answer with one word: *adaption* – a necessary and reasonable adaption to the basic requirements of modern, science-based, and institutionally differentiated societies in crisis. And this applies to us all, religious and non-religious, but *also* to the religious, in different variations, in accordance with what we have mentioned previously. Here, summarized in three points:

---

1 As Habermas sees it, see the chapter above.
2 As Samuel Huntington sees it, cf. the classic: *The Clash of Civilizations and the Remaking of World Order*, from 1996.

DOI: 10.4324/9781003441618-12

Religion in science-based and institutionally differentiated **109**

- Epistemic requirements. We must, in a reasonable fashion, based on our own circumstances and capabilities, as individuals and communities,[3] live up to the complex knowledge-related challenges of modern science-based societies – as they have been outlined previously. Two reminders: (i) This involves an openness towards enlightened discussion, towards the exchange of opinions and possible counterarguments, and towards alternative perspectives and preconditions. In short, we must not become "argumentophobe"! (ii) It involves, by extension, that we must not disregard or reject relevant alternative perspectives that raise critical questions about our own principles and convictions – be it questions related to culture and society, power and politics, or nature and biological conditions for life. In short, we must not be "semi-modern", in the sense that we shy away from certain kinds of scientific and scholarly insights!
- Institutional requirements. Here, there are challenges at two levels: (i) a political and societal task, to implement modern and functioning institutions, each on their own and in relation to each other, and (ii) a personal task, to act and behave in accordance with the requirements posed by the different institutions. This, e.g., means that we distinguish between private roles in our family life and professional roles in the work sphere, and between private roles and roles in the public sphere. For instance, within the family, we give our children special treatment, but our uncle's children are not to receive special treatment when we are members of a public admission committee, and in private contexts, we may indicate our religious orientation, e.g., with hijab of a kippa, but not as a legal judge or as a uniformed police officer in service.
- Crises. Faced with the many complex and often intertwined challenges of our time, the aforementioned knowledge-related and institutional challenges often become pressing and urgent, for us all, religious as well as non-religious. A couple of points in this regard: Faced with such complex challenges, an "ethics of conviction" (*Gesinnungsetik*) is not a morally responsible standpoint. Neither is it ethically justifiable to rely on ethical doctrines from an earlier point in history, with other challenges, and quite different epistemic and institutional preconditions.[4] In such cases, what is needed is an epistemically and institutionally updated "consequentialism" which takes into consideration the complexity of the challenges and the expected outcomes of our actions, both on a short-term and on a long-term basis.

---

3 This should include, e.g., high-quality basic education for all, founded by the state. Cf. my comments on education in Gunnar Skirbekk, *Epistemic Challenges in a Modern World*, LIT Verlag, Zürich, 2019.
4 The Old Testament and Sharia cannot be expected to provide reasonable normative guidance in the face of complex modern challenges.

110 Religion in modern societies

But "religion" may also be a *resource* in modern societies in crisis. Ambiguously, true enough, and with a need for adapting, as is the case for us all, but also as something potentially positive, based on various perspectives.[5] In closing, we will accentuate three points that tend to be disregarded in many contexts where socio-political or socio-cultural issues are favoured:

- *A sense of wonder*, existentially and cosmologically. In short, religiousness, not in the shape of answers, but rather as questions. Simply, a sense of wonder. The wonder of being here, as a person, in the midst of it all.[6] But also of cosmos. That it is. Overwhelming and unfathomable.[7]
- *Theology*. As enlightened reflection and serious discussion about the grand questions, from the proof of God in Thomas Aquinas to the discussion of the problem of evil in Leibniz or Hans Jonas, or in newer versions, in light of recent research and philosophy, as in Peter Rohs.[8]
- *The religious language* may be many things, from bad rhetoric to frivolous talk. But not only. Just as "there is a time for everything", to cite the Ecclesiastes in the Holy Bible, there are languages for many things. Language for grief, language for wondering. Language in writing, and language as speech acts, and thus contextual, dependent on the situation. And then we come close to the ritual, and the particularities of different places and spaces, where song, and the act of singing together, belongs. But also as a language that communicates specific attitudes towards life that lives – that expresses an awe for life, for living life, as Albert Schweitzer wanted it, and perhaps also Arne Næss, with his deep ecology. Yes, legally and morally, respect for human beings, for weird and vulnerable human beings! But more than that: respect and awe for vulnerable life.[9] Simple as that.

Religion in modern societies? Yes, when reasonably adapted, religion belongs in human life as it is, wondrous and vulnerable. So religion, in this sense, will be with us, as long as we are here.

---

5 As, e.g., Habermas emphasises.

6 As a basic feature of existential philosophy and in poetry.

7 "Not how the world is, but that it is, is the mystery" (*Nicht wie die Welt ist, ist das Mystische, sondern dass sie ist*) Ludwig Wittgenstein, *Logisch-Philosophische Abhandlung* (*Tractatus logico-philosophicus*), proposition 6.44.

8 Metaphysics, perhaps? But if so, then, not all current philosophy is "post-metaphysical"! (References to Leibniz, Hans Jonas and Peter Rohs have been provided above.)

9 Cf. thoughts on religious language, in Gunnar Skirbekk, *Den filosofiske uroa*, Universitetsforlaget, Oslo 2005, pp. 171–183.

INFO ON PREVIOUS WORK

For general information, see homepages,
http://www.uib.no/personer/Gunnar.Skirbekk#
http://gunnarskirbekk.no/
with references to relevant articles and books;
in English, for instance:

Nihilism? A Young Man's Search for Meaning (Bergen 1972). Original version: *Nihilisme? Eit ungt menneskes forsøk på å orientere seg* (Oslo 1958).

Rationality and Modernity. Essays in Philosophical Pragmatics (Oslo/Oxford 1993).

A History of Western Thought, From ancient Greece to the twentieth century (London/New York 2001), together with Nils Gilje. Published in 18 languages; original version: *Filosofihistorie* (eighth edition, Oslo 2007).

Timely Thoughts. Modern Challenges and Philosophical Responses: Contributions to Inter-Cultural Dialogues (Lanham 2007).

Multiple Modernities. A Tale of Scandinavian Experiences (Hong Kong 2011).

Notes in retrospect, for my Chinese friends (Bergen 2013).

Epistemic Challenges in a Modern World. From 'fake news' and 'post truth' to underlying epistemic challenges in science-based risk-societies (Zürich 2019).

INDEX

Pages followed by n refer notes.

Abraham 88; Abrahamic 21
Adorno, Theodor 21n4
Ahmadinejad, Mahmoud 16
al-Kubaisi, Walid 57
Apel, Karl-Otto 79, 80n15, 90n67
argumentophobia 4, 4n5;
   argumentophobe 109
Aristotelian 13–14, 87–88
Arnason, Johann 59n5
Asad, Talal 68n42, 71n53
Augustine 20, 24n14, 87
Atatürk, Mustafa Kemal 99n5, 107
Ayer, Alfred 15n34

Bacon, Francis 16n38, 88
Bagge, Sverre 105n28
Bangstad, Sindre 68n38
Barry, Brian 57n2
Bellah, Robert 94, 94n91
Bergman, Ingmar 84n37
Berkeley, George 88
Billeskov Jansen, Frederik Julius 54n3
blasphemy 19, 30, 33; unintended
   blasphemy 19, 71n51, 71n53
blasphemous 20, 29n29, 33;
   unintentionally blasphemous 33
Bloch, Ernst 25n18
Bringeland, Hans xn1, 57n1
Brown, Wendy 68n42

Brunvoll, Arve xn1
Burke, Edmund 41
Butler, Judith 68n42

Castberg, Johan 60, 106n34
Cicourel, Aron 25n18
clan loyalty 58
Comte, Auguste 15
Confucius 87
critique of religion 12–16, 49–50
critique of science 4–6
Cronin, Ciaran 77n2, 77n4

Darwin, Charles 16n38, 41n7, 107
Dehly, Axel Gerhard 106n31
Descartes, René 88
Dreyfus, Hubert 12n28
Durkheim, Émile 14n32, 86n51, 94,
   94n91, 94n92
Døving, Alexa 68n38

Eder, Klaus 78n7
Eisenstadt, Shmuel 87n55
Ekeland, Anders 62n16
epistemic 8, 8n18, 9; gradualistic
   epistemically 8n17; melioristic
   epistemically 8n17
Erdogan, Recep Tayyip 99n4
Eriksen, Erik Oddvar 63n19, 70n47

Index **113**

Fet, Jostein 101n12
Flyberg, Lis 101n12
Freud, Sigmund 14, 22n7, 25n18, 41n7, 107
Frey, Carl Benedikt 62n16
Fukuyama, Francis 105, 105n29

Galileo Galilei 14
Gambetta, Diego 26n20
Garrett, Fydell Edmund 106n31
Gautama, Siddharta Buddha 87
Gelasius 24n14
Ghaly, Mohammed 101n11
Ghazali 102, 102n18, 102n19, 102n21
Gilje, Nils xn1, 13n31, 80n16, 85n41, 99n7, 102n20, 106n31, 111
Gutenberg, Johann 100

Habermas, Jürgen xn2, 14n32, 15n33, 17n43, 31n33, 32, 45n11, 67n34, 68, 68n42, 69n42, 77–96, 104, 104n27, 108n1, 110n5
Haddad, Shaykh Gibril 28n26
Hannay, Alastair 92n85
Hallesby, Ole 21n5
Hauge, Hans Nielsen 69n45, 105, 106n31, 107
Hegel, Georg Wilhelm Friedrich 21, 41, 85, 85n42, 89; Hegelian 89, 89n64, 90
Heidegger, Martin 12n28, 85, 85n42
Hempel, Carl 4n3
Henrich, Joseph 105n30
Herder, Johann Gottfried von 89
Hertog, Steffen 26n20
Hitler, Adolf 72n54, 84n37
Hobbes, Thomas 40–41
Holberg, Ludvig 54, 95n95
Holmøy, Erling 61n12
Hommerstad, Marthe 106n32
Hume, David 16n39, 88, 89n63
Huntington, Samuel 108n2
Husserl, Edmund 85, 85n42

ibn Arqam, Zayd 28n26
ibn Sinâ Avicenna 102n21
Ibsen, Henrik 105, 106n31
Isaac 88

Janicaud, Dominique 12n28
Jaspers, Karl 87, 87n54
Jesus 22–23, 33; Christ 22, 25, 33

Johannessen, Kjell S. 79n12
Johansen, Anders 106n32, 107n36
Jonas, Hans 21, 21n5, 25n18, 27n21, 28n24, 90n70, 110, 110n8

Kant, Immanuel 16, 16n36, 20, 20n3, 67n36, 85n41, 88–89, 89n63
Kantian 11n26, 18, 18n45, 50, 68, 84, 90n70
Kepel, Gilles 70n50
Kierkegaard, Søren 80n16, 89
Kildal, Nanna 58n3, 60n10
Kokkvold, Per Edgar 39n4
Kuhnle, Stein 58n3, 60n10
Kuru, Ahmet T. 17n42, 24n14, 25n16, 50n14, 95n93, 97–107
Kurzweil, Raymond 93n87
Kymlicka, William 57n2

Langvatn, Silje Aambø 66n32
Lanier, Jaron 6n8
Latour, Bruno 12n28
Leibniz, Gottfried Wilhelm 20, 20n2, 27n23, 33, 40n6, 88, 90n70, 110n8
Leirvik, Oddbjørn 68n38
Lidegaard, Bo 72n54
Locke, John 40, 41, 88
Loftager, Jørn 63n19, 70n47
Lund-Olsen, Tone 3n1
Luther, Martin 24n14, 28n25, 78n9, 87, 87n59, 88, 88n60, 100
Lutheran 59, 60n8, 69, 105–107

Matthew 84n40
Marsilius 24n14
Marcuse, Herbert 25n18
Marx, Karl 14, 25n18, 89; Marxist 21
Materstvedt, Lars Johan 4n5
Mendelsohn, Moses 25n18
Mendieta, Eduardo 69n42
Merton, Robert 7n11
Mill, John Stuart 7n12, 42
Mitchell, P. M. 54n3, 54n4, 95n95
modernity x, xn2, 17, 59n7, 78n10
modernization of consciousness 16–18, 45, 48n13, 50, 67–68, 71, 96, 96n96
Muhammed 37–38, 45, 48–50, 53, 102n22; the Prophet 24, 26, 38, 47, 49, 53
Münkler, Herfried 95n94

114 Index

Nasser, Gamal Abdel 99n5
Newton, Isaac 16n38, 89
Nietzsche, Friedrich 14, 41n7
Næss, Arne 92n85, 110

Ockham, William 24n14, 87
offence two concepts 52–54
O'Neill, Onora 9n19
Orning, Hans Jacob 95n94
Osborne, Michael A. 62n16

Pajarinen, Mika 62n16
Pascal, Blaise 88, 88n62
Peirce, Charles Sanders 89, 89n64
Plato 33, 40n6, 87; Platonic, Platonism 13, 20, 87
Plesner, Ingvill Thorson 68n38
Plotinus 87
Polanyi, Michael 79n12
Popper, Karl 6

Qutb, Sayyid 16, 16n37, 26n20

Rana, Mohammad Usman 30n32
Rasmussen, Tarald 106n31
Rawls, John 17n44, 32n35, 38n2, 68n41, 68n42
Rohs, Peter 15n35, 18n46, 68n40, 69n42, 90n70, 110, 110n8
Rouvinen, Petri 62n16
Russell, Bertrand 92n84

Saba, Mahmood 68n42
Sachs, Jeffrey 62n17
Schjelderup, Kristian 21n5
Schweitzer, Albert 27n21, 110
semi-modern 6, 16, 109; semi-modernization 26n20

Shapin, Steven 13n30
Skjervheim, Hans 84n40
Snow, Charles Percy 65, 65n28
Soelvold, Peder 106n32
Sophie Charlotte 20
Spinoza, Baruch de 25n18, 88
Strøm, Birger 61n12
Stråth, Bo 59n5, 60n11
Sørensen, Øystein 59n5, 60n11
Søvik, Atle Ottesen 21n6

Taner, Edis 26n20
Taylor, Charles 68n42
Tetens, Holm 15n35
Thomas Aquinas 20, 24n14, 28n25, 87, 110
Tomasello, Michael 82, 82n30, 86n52
Troyel, Isaac 20n2

Vaage, Nora Sørensen 3n1
validity claims 16, 19, 48n13, 63, 71n53, 91
VanAntwerpen, Jonathan 69n42
Voltaire, François-Marie Arouet 14, 16n39, 20

Weber, Max xn2, 78n10
Wergeland, Henrik 106n32
Witoszek, Nina 60n11
Wittgenstein, Ludwig 79n12, 110n7
Wittrock, Björn 59n5

Østerud, Øyvind 95n94
Øyen, Simen Andersen 3n1

Yu, Zhenhua 79n12

Printed in the USA
CPSIA information can be obtained
at www.ICGtesting.com
LVHW021736041124
795688LV00040B/1270